Built to be CEO

To Mama and Dada –

who put my success
before their own

&

To Tim Condon –

who taught me everything
that Harvard did not teach me.

Built to be CEO

.

A special thank you to those who supported this research project that has evolved into this book.

There are too many to name, but I will try. Thank you to my encouraging family (Shamira Ghouse, Arushka Theagarajah, Jade Lu and of course, my incredible grandmother Faiza "Umma" Mansoor), to my middle school and high school support circles (Anithra Basnayake, Mrs. Elizabeth Moir, Maneesha Gunatilleka, Maalavika Manoj, Nadia Mathew, Tashi Shearer, Ureshka Fernando, all my wonderful teachers, and so many more), to my incredible achievers from Harvard College (Adrienne Simes, Amanda Milunovich, Amy Jiang, Annie Garofalo, Aya Darwazeh, Chisom Okpala, Chloe George, Disha Verma, Deirdre Buckley, Lindsay Mailer-Howat, Megan Reynolds, McKenna Kardish, and so many more), to my inner circle of incredible women in the San Francisco Bay Area (Alexis Davis, Ananda Baron, Arushi Jain, Beth Vasquez, Carole-eden Sylvester, Cindy Kaczmarek, Dani Doroff, Desiree Navarro, Donna Diaz, Esther Stine, Jennifer Botterill, Kamili Moreland, Karen Bianchini, Laura Furstenthal, Laura Zeigler, Marianne Campbell, Meg Vrabel, Monica Alejandre, Natasha Miller, Nicolette Zalesky, Patti, Lee, Rachel Escoto, Rachael Radu, Ryley Reynolds, Sarah Abrams, Sarah Swigart, Sue Hagen, Suna Taymaz, Tasha Tolbert, Tena Melfi, Victoria Tinsley, Viviane Ford, and many more).
Thank you to Harvard Business Review, Forbes, The New York Times, Korn Ferry and other publications that have invested in researching the power of women in the workplace. Thank you to all those who wrote blogs, research papers and theses – you fueled many of the recommendations in this book.
And THANK YOU to Atul Bhattarai for editing my work over the course of over a year, and to Marcella Murillo for hearing about the project, seeing the bigger picture in this book and offering to design the cover.

Built to be CEO

In my short career, I have worn many hats and served many CEOs, mostly as a Chief of Staff. In this role, I learned lessons about building a strong resume, finding a solid support network, embodying situational leadership, practicing self-awareness, maintaining drive and building a unique brand to advance your career. I will share the most important ones with you — the ones that pertain to creating future CEOs.

I will admit, I want to be a CEO one day, and I know it will not be a smooth journey there. For those of you who have considered aiming for the role — whether you identify as a woman or not — I am here to validate your goals and provide you with advanced career advice on how to get there. For those of you who have not thought about or decided how you would like your career to develop, I am here to convince you that you are built to be a CEO.

Built to be CEO

Introduction
You Haven't Come this Far Just to Come this Far

You, like me, are proud of having achieved at least one thing in your life you set out to do. You defined a goal. You asked yourself, "What do I need to accomplish?" and "Why am I doing what I'm doing?" You probably crafted a plan or process for achieving your goal – "When must I do it?" and "How well must I do it?" You may have even tracked your performance – "How am I doing?"

But have you asked yourself, "Is there more I can do?" or "Can I do better, and go further?" Have you asked yourself, "am I built for more?"

Because the answer is YES. You are built to be at the top of the food chain.

Everyone around you sets goals for themselves. But you may also be surrounded by people ready to conquer another jungle – the business world. And once in a while, you will stumble across a different, rarer kind of Alpha: a future CEO.

Future CEOs will accomplish more in their careers than the average person. They consistently ask themselves, "Is there more I can do? Can I do better? Am I built for more?" and they answer their own questions undoubtedly with, "yes." While we all set goals, future CEOs continue to push the boundaries of their goals and remind themselves that they *haven't come this far just to come this far.*

You may have heard people refer to CEOs as certain types of animals. In my opinion, in today's world, a typical CEO reflects a striking physical and behavioral resemblance to a male North American moose. These creatures are the tallest mammals in North America, are one of the deadliest to humans who cannot protect themselves, maintain striking postures in their environments and have deep, strong voices. Similarly, the typical chief executive is more than six feet tall, has a deep voice, a sturdy posture and can be deadly to those who are not prepared to interact with *him*.

In our jungle, a chief executive officer (CEO) is the highest-ranking executive in a company, responsible for making major corporate decisions, managing the overall operations and resources of a company and acting as the main point of communication between the board of directors and corporate operations. While the typical CEO may look like a North American moose, the typical physical characteristics of a *future* CEO can be shaped by you.

When I first introduced the visual of CEOs resembling the North American moose to my mentor Laura Furstenthal, she laughed and said, "well, that makes female CEOs unicorns!" Unicorns, not in a *one-in-a-million* or a *sparkles-and-rainbow-hair* kind of way, but in that female CEOs are special.

The purpose of this book is to, at the very least, remind young women that women are built to be CEOs. The Korn Ferry Institute's study on when women "realized they could be CEO" shows that 65% attributed this realization to someone telling them they *could be* a CEO.[1] The finding implied that the primary driver for creating future female CEOs is to tell more women that becoming a CEO is possible. The research also noted that 16% said it became clear only when they reached a higher role and only 12% said they had wanted this position for a long time.[i]

"Why not me?" is a phrase Jennifer Botterill, four-time Olympic Hockey medalist, five-time World Champion and twice-named MVP, taught me. Jennifer empowered me to use this phrase more often; it is one that has become my answer to many questions. I have used this phrase so much that it has morphed from a rhetorical question into a robust statement. Why are you presenting? *Why not me.* Who will be CEO? *Why not me.*

So, why not you?

I will admit, I am not a CEO – yet. In fact, I am the first woman in my family to attend college and I owe it to my mother, Shahareen, who encouraged me to be what I was built to be. My mother's great grandfather, Segu Ismail Lebbe Marikar Abdul Caffoor Marikar–Hadjiar, received an MBE for his social service work in 1952, on behalf of King George VI of England. Her father was a doctor, who used his education to open a medical dispensary for low-income members of his community. Her two brothers went to medical school and business school, and now enjoy successful careers in the UK. But Shahareen did not get her high school diploma. Why? Apparently, when she was prepared to pursue her education and a competitive career, women were not expected to go to college.

---

[1] This statistic imprinted on me because if I were to become CEO in the future, I would be in this category.

11

In fact, no one in my family is a CEO. However, I have worked for more than one in a close capacity, as an Executive Analyst and as a Manager of Enterprise Analytics for the Executive Team. In this role, I interacted frequently with the CEO, a former CEO and executives of a multi-billion dollar company to execute cross-functional priority projects. These projects impacted a range of people – thousands of employees to millions of citizens. I also served for years as a CEO's Chief of Staff, where I learned the most about what it takes to operate as a successful CEO. It was also the experience that presented the most opportunities to interact with CEOs from multiple industries in business meetings. After I moved on from the Chief of Staff role, I joined a CEO's Advisory Cabinet, which consisted of a few trusted Members empowered to advise the CEO on decisions and other matters that pertained to operating the company.

Where I can, I will share my experiences – but this book is about you and your journey. The next chapters will take you through the obstacles you may face, the skills you will need to pick up and the paths you may take to make it to the top.

I will also feature stories from five role models, mentors and sponsors. **Patti Lee**, an Emmy-winning reporter and one of my performance coaches, provided me with continuous support and reminders that I *am* a future CEO. **Jennifer Botterill**, a four-time Olympic medalist and another one of my performance coaches, consistently reminds me of the "why not me?" mindset. **Alexis Davis**, an Ultimate Fighting Champion, assured me that I should not care about what others think, and that sometimes I will need to fight *myself* to get to where I deserve to be. **Laura Furstenthal**, a managing partner at McKinsey with a PhD in cancer biology, provided me with the research and energy that became the foundation for many of the facts and figures I will share with you. **Shahareen Ghouse**, my mother and a lifelong teacher, encouraged me to move 10,000 miles away from home to pursue my dreams.

I hope that soon the message that this book holds will become obsolete because it is commonplace to see women in CEO positions across every industry.

The Building Blocks for CEOs

Chapter 1: Do You Want to be CEO?

The CEO position could be for you. One of the primary factors in connecting women to the CEO position, according to studies, is being told that it is possible to be a CEO. By becoming CEO, you could change some disappointing trends – only 6.4% of Fortune 500 companies were run by female CEOs in 2017, which is 15 times fewer women than men.

Chapter 2: Time is Your Most Valuable Player (MVP)

Time is a resource far more valuable than money. Women, in many instances, are not equally compensated as men for their time. Using your time effectively in your early career to build your upward trajectory and fulfill your aspirational goals could transform and accelerate your path to CEO.

Understand What You're Getting Into

Chapter 3: The Force Fields in Your Environment

Biochemistry may not be holding women back from being CEO, but Hollywood could be a contributing factor starting from childhood. The industry limits female succession planning through its pervasive stereotypes and shortage of role models.

Chapter 4: The Types and Traits of CEOs

There are a number of key personality traits that future CEOs must develop to accelerate their career, align their personal goals with their professional goals and embody successful traits early on.

Chapter 5: A List of Excuses

I have dedicated this chapter to listing excuses, because I want to ensure they do not obstruct you from becoming a CEO.

Start Your Training Early

Chapter 6: The Resume Builder

There are not too many technical skills required to become CEO, versus personality and leadership skills. What is non-negotiable is a deep understanding of and some experience in corporate finance.

Chapter 7: The Agenda Drivers

In business, you are going to need to know how to convince people about yourself and your ideas. You will need to learn how to establish trust, change the conversation, pay attention to body language, anticipate criticism, be aware of your biases and dispel stereotypes about women.

Chapter 8: The Support Boosters

You do not have to travel alone on your path to the top of the pyramid. Find your mentors, sponsors and supporters early on in your career and pay their support forward to other young women who could benefit from learning from you.

Chapter 9: The Cherry on Top

While men tend to remove junior-level roles from their LinkedIn profiles, women publish 11% fewer skills than men. It is time for women to build unique personal brands and advertise the value they add to their workplace, industry and community.

Chapter 10: Your Path(s) Forward

Your path to becoming a CEO is unique to you, and influenced by three key questions. Do you value your experience or education more? Do you prefer to travel on or off the beaten path? When do you want to be CEO?

Conclusion: Surgite

Chapter 1
Do You Want to be CEO?

I don't know. Probably not. Maybe?

What do the numbers say?

Well, the businesses listed on the S&P 500 run by women are outperforming those run by their male counterparts. These businesses generated a median total shareholder return of *18.4%* in 2016, compared with *15.7%* for those run by men.

Moreover, female chief executives at some of the largest U.S. companies, such as those on the S&P 500, are offered higher compensation packages and repeatedly out-earn their male counterparts. In 2017, 21 female CEOs received a median compensation package of *$13.8 million*, compared with *$11.6 million* for 382 male chiefs.[ii]

This stretches beyond the S&P 500 into middle-market companies, which account for the middle third of the U.S. economy. At these companies, in 2018, close to one in three female-led companies targeted and achieved growth rates that exceeded *15%* for the year, compared to just *5%* at male-led firms. This was despite more than half the women-led companies saying they had no access to external funding.[iii]

Despite delivering better financial performance and being compensated for it, women are underrepresented in leadership positions across industries. While women represented nearly half of the world's population in 2018, only 4.8% of Fortune 500 companies were run by female CEOs.

That's ridiculous.

It gets even more ridiculous. In fact, it is actually as easy to find a man named John as it is to find a woman in the corridors of American power. According to a New York Times piece from April 2018, fewer Republican senators are women than men named John – despite the fact that Johns represent 3.3% of the male population. Fewer Democratic governors are women than men named John. Let's throw names like Michael, David, Daniel and James into the mix. Fewer women directed the top-grossing 100 films in 2017 than men named Michael and James.[iv]

Republican Senators	Democratic Govenors	Cabinet Members	Presidents of Colleges
• 12% women • 14% men named John	• 13% women • 19% men named John	• 21% women • 25% men named John, Daniel, David and James	• 21% women • 23% men named John, David, James, Richard, Robert, Thomas and William

Clearly, these statistics are not acceptable, given the number of women in the world. They certainly do not do justice to the female potential for high performance in the business world.

So, what do the numbers say? That there is room at the top of the business world for more women. More women need to rise to become CEOs.

Are the numbers improving for women?
Over time, yes. At some point, there were zero female CEOs at Fortune 500 companies. In 2018, there were around 25 more.

Number of Females in Fortune 500

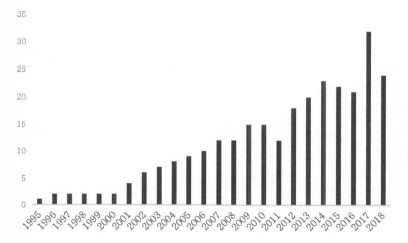

In fact, 2017 was an exciting year – the proportion of women leading companies in the Fortune 500 had grown to 6.4%, a record high from 2.6% a decade earlier. In 2018, however, the proportion of female chief executives *declined* to 4.8%. This was a 25% decline between 2017 and 2018. Of these, 12 left their jobs and four joined the list.

Out of the 12 who left, four said they were retiring; four left after their companies were acquired; two took new jobs, and two were replaced after calls for change from investors.

Among the hundreds of men on the list, a much smaller share left – only 47. And when women leave the top job, there are fewer women in the pipeline to take their place; women hold only 21% of feeder roles for CEO, like the senior-vice-president position.[v] In each of the 12 cases above in which a new or interim chief executive was appointed, the woman was replaced by a man.[vi] THIS is why we need more women in the pipeline for executive-level positions that lead up to being elected to the CEO role.

So, the numbers are not improving?

The numbers are improving slowly. So slowly that you can barely see the progress over a 30-year period.

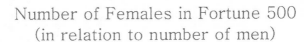

Number of Females in Fortune 500
(in relation to number of men)

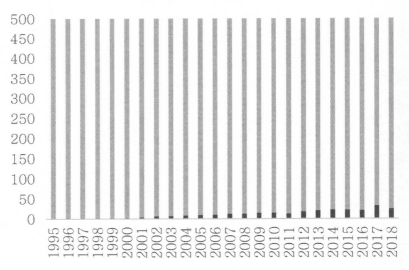

Why so slowly? A study by Paysa found that 41% of women surveyed could not muster the courage to ask for a raise. A study by Harvard Business Review showed that women tend to apply for jobs only if they meet 100% of the qualifications, whereas men do so when they meet only 60%.[vii] Of female respondents, 42% were denied raises, compared with 33% of male respondents in another survey.

There is unlikely to be one root cause to explain why fewer than 5% of Fortune 500 companies have female CEOs. More importantly, the number of female CEOs will not grow on its own. We must address the factors behind it. Some are more passive, like fostering an environment that empowers women to strive to become CEO. Others are active for you, and require you to alter your career trajectory.

What do CEOs do, anyway?
CEO stands for Chief Executive Officer.

- **The CEO owns the vision** – She determines and communicates the organization's strategic direction, which all other decisions are based on. Without this, the company is merely a collection of humans pursuing individual goals, guided by their own values.
- **The CEO balances resources** – She controls three of the corporate world's most important resources – capital, people and *her time* – to drive the company's success.
- **The CEO strengthens the culture** – She establishes and shares the set of shared attitudes, goals, behaviors and values that characterize the group of people that represents the company.
- **The CEO makes the decisions** – While some final decisions may be up to the CEO's boss (the Board of Directors), she uses the vision, sources and culture she has established to execute strategy and deliver performance.

The Korn Ferry Institute interviewed 57 women CEOs in November 2017 – from 41 Fortune 1000 companies and 16 large, privately held companies. Four key findings emerged:

1. They were driven by both a sense of purpose and a desire to achieve business results. Almost 25% pointed to creating a positive culture as their most successful achievement.
2. The most prominent traits that sustained their success on the road to CEO were courage, risk-taking, resilience, agility and managing ambiguity.
3. They were more likely to engage the power of teams, scoring significantly higher than the benchmark on humility and their expression of gratitude for others.
4. The women shared STEM (Science, Technology, Engineering, Mathematics) and finance backgrounds that served as a springboard for their careers – 40% had extensive experience in STEM and 19% in finance.[viii]

What does this have to do with me?

What would you attempt in your career if you knew you could not fail? If you have not decided exactly what you want out of your career, the CEO position might be for you. The position does not dictate which industry you must commit to. It is flexible in accommodating your interests. It also comes with some benefits that are difficult to turn down. For example:

1. *Exceptional exposure to unlimited learning opportunities and incredibly high-achieving people.* A CEO typically knows more about a company's state of affairs than anyone else. Because of her position, the CEO is more likely to be informed about market conditions and the economic state of the business environment. She also has the gravitas to seek knowledge from experts in any industry.
2. *The unmatched ability to make an impact.* Within a company, the CEO is usually the top decision maker,

allowing for a significant amount of control over the way a business functions. A CEO typically has authority over financial decisions, people decisions, strategic planning and overall company direction. Depending on the extent to which her brand is tied to being the CEO of the company, she could extend her impact into her community and other lines of work. For example, she could join and contribute to community or charity organizations, or start her own; she could become a board member of an organization in a different industry to add diverse business perspectives.

3. *Some pretty nice perks.* The title of CEO usually comes with a higher earning potential than any other position. Even after the U.S. financial collapse that began in 2008, CEOs still enjoyed high salaries, as they continued to be the main decision-makers in setting the strategy for the company to get through rough financial times. According to The Corporate Library, the annual compensation for CEOs rose in 2009 to an average of $1.1 million per year. In general, over 51% of organizations offer additional performance bonuses to their CEOs; a quarter of these reported that other staff did not enjoy this benefit. CEOs also often enjoy benefits of leadership through company perks, which may include taking home a share of the company's annual profits. They also may have access to expense and entertainment accounts, as well as business property for use, including cars and houses. CEOs may also receive lucrative retirement packages, post-retirement consulting contracts and other extras not typically available to lower-level employees. CEOs are expensive, and it is more fun to be one and enjoy the perks that come with the role than to have to report to one.

In addition to what you get out of being a CEO, you are playing an *active* role in balancing the representation of females to males at the top of the corporate pyramid. Your journey to CEO could foster an environment where more young women feel confident to say, "I could be a CEO one day." So, if you have not said it yet, go ahead – say it: "I am built to be a CEO."

Isn't it too early to say that?

No, it is not too early to say you are built to be a CEO, or act like a future CEO. It might be days, months, years or decades until you become a CEO, based on the foundation you have laid for your career and decisions you make for yourself. The important tidbit to remember here is that you charter your own journey. This book will help you shape yours to lead to the CEO position. Moreover, you may need to start early to gather the skills needed to be a successful CEO.

I began working for a CEO of a multi-billion dollar enterprise right out of college. I learned every day that I do not yet have the skills to be a CEO. I have highlighted in this book the skills, traits and experiences that build successful CEOs. And because I am yet to work for a company with a female CEO, my experience has served as a reminder that there is certainly room for more women in leadership positions.

But it is true that most CEOs fall into a particular age range. Harvard Business Review published research that indicates the business world believes the peak age for good financial decision-making is 53 years.[ix] A survey of 158 senior business executives found that 47% would not hire a qualified 72-year-old as CEO and only 4% would hire a qualified 47-year-old as CEO.[x] This preference in age range for CEOs plays out in reality. Of S&P 500 CEOs, only 5.4% are 47 and younger, and only 1.2% are 72 and older.

Even within the preferred CEO age range, the average age of a CEO skews older. The average age for a CEO across industries is 58; the highest average is 60, in financial services, and the lowest is 55, in the technology sector.[xi] Even in the tech industry, the age of entrepreneurs is rising. At the Founders Institute, a Mountain View–based startup incubator, the average age of its 330 enrolled participants in 2013 was 35; it was 29 when Founders Institute began in 2009. At TechStars, another influential tech incubator, the average age of its current crop of founders was around 32, up from about 25 several years ago.[xii]

Additionally, despite a decrease in average tenure, the average age of a CEO is increasing across industries. The average age of new CEOs in the Fortune 500 and S&P 500 has increased since 2012, climbing from 45 to 50. Companies are encouraging this trend. While firms such as Altria and General Electric encourage CEOs to retire by 65, 67% of 400 senior executives surveyed are campaigning for no mandatory retirement age. So, that ideal CEO age range could move further out, even as you get older – it is a good thing that humans are living longer!

So my journey starts now, but I need to wait *years* to be a CEO?

Your journey starts as soon as you say, out loud, "I am built to be a CEO." Believing you can be a future CEO is the start of a journey that you charter. Your timeline rests on the choices you make on your journey.

It is certainly possible to perform at a high level despite being younger than the ideal age range. The youngest executive on Harvard Business Review's list of the 100 Best Performing CEOs in 2014 was Simon Wolfson of *Next*, at age 46. According to HBR's research on age and innovation, even he may be past his creative peak; the research shows that the peak age for great innovation falls between *35 to 45*.[xiii]

As more young people are empowered to start their own companies and innovate, maybe the ideal CEO age range will be seen as nothing but an old social construct. Perhaps it *is* time to move away from the image of the six foot North American moose in a corner office, and towards a fresh perspective with younger and more diverse leaders.

The numbers would support this: the S&P 500 companies run by the youngest CEOs have been outperforming those run by the oldest.

- Of the 27 CEOs of S&P 500 who are 47 and younger, 23 have been CEO since the start of 2007. Those 23 stocks are down an average 2.8% over 19 months vs. a 9% decline in the S&P 500 index.
- The stocks of six companies with CEOs who are 72 and older are down an average of 21%.[xiv]

Female CEOs are not the same age as their average male counterparts. A study with 12,000 observations conducted over 15 years indicates that that female CEOs are younger on average by approximately two full years than male CEOs (after controlling for firm and board characteristics).[xv] That's as much as 26% of the standard deviation in CEO age.

So, although the world as it exists today paints the picture of what a typical CEO looks like and how old *he* should be, the world might be ready for a fresh perspective. These averages should not be considered requirements for the role. Additionally, the typical CEO will change over time. Your age should not deter you to from aiming for the CEO seat now. In fact, it should motivate you to start early; be aware that the journey might be a long one, but that it is absolutely possible to outperform CEOs in the ideal age range.

What next?

The path to CEO is not an easy one and the next few chapters will inform you what you are getting into. You will likely encounter force fields in your environment that make it difficult for you to succeed. You will need to focus on developing specific personality traits.

While doing this, you might be tempted to excuse yourself from the path to the top. The chapters that follow will teach you what you need to be successful. Corporate finance experience is a must, and *Chapter 6: The Resume Builder* will guide you through the financial decisions you may need to make when running a company. You will also need drive, a unique brand and supporters – topics I will cover in Chapters 7, 8 and 9.

I will also run you through the possible paths to get to the CEO seat. These lessons are informed by my experience working closely with multiple CEOs from different educational and experiential backgrounds.

But first, the next chapter will dive into how to value time in your early career, as we build your path(s) to CEO.

You want to be a CEO?

Take some advice from a trailblazer who directly addressed gender bias in a world full of "Johns" – Drew Faust. Faust was Harvard's first female President. I was fortunate enough to meet her during my freshman year of college. During her appointment in 2007, she said:

> It's really important that I inhabit this role··· [My appointment] has an important symbolic force within American life, American higher education, and even around the world··· I'm not the woman president of Harvard. I'm the President of Harvard. [xvi]

Like Drew Faust, I hope that one day the appointment of a woman as CEO is so common that it's no longer noteworthy. And I am confident that your journey can contribute to this.

Chapter 2
Early Career –
Time is Your MVP

If you want to be CEO, you have competition. More people are positioning themselves to be future business leaders than ever before. More Americans are attending college than ever before – nearly 90% of millennials who graduate from high school attend college within eight years.[xvii] Educational institutions are curating courses to groom future CEOs, such as the University of Pennsylvania's Wharton Global CEO Program. Companies might still behind the trend: only two-thirds of US public and private companies still admit that they have no formal CEO succession plan in place and only one-third of the executives headhunted by the Korn Ferry Institute claimed their companies had young CEO training programs.[xviii] Nevertheless, leadership rotations are becoming a more common practice and succession plans are becoming more tailored to plan for building future CEOs. Your most valuable player (MVP) to get to the top is *time*. Start early and use your time wisely.

The Chief of Staff (to the CEO) role taught me the value of time in my early career. A Chief of Staff will calculate the value of a CEO's time and ensure it is preserved at minimum, and ideally enhanced over time.

A Chief of Staff's (COS) sole responsibility, as a catch-all position, is to make the CEO's life easier. This often means success in this role is measured by how much of the CEO's time a COS saves, so the CEO can focus on developing and achieving the company's bigger picture vision.

I committed over 80 hours a week for three years to the Chief of Staff role, where I spent almost all of my time with the CEO of a multi-billion dollar company or working on projects that would move the needle for him. This involved, but is not limited to, building his brand by writing speeches and making his presentations, conveying information and speaking on his behalf at meetings, contributing to the documents he presented to the Board of Directors and researching organizations to partner with or acquire. I learned how to work in 12 hour cycles – all requests and most projects would be completed 12 hours or fewer (my current non-CEO team complains about this work-style that I have not been able to abandon yet!). My tasks were bucketed into four time horizons based on how long I had to complete them – one week, one day, one hour and *one minute.*

The 12,000 hours spent in close contact with the CEO I worked for, as well as other CEOs he interacted frequently with, provided me with a wealth of knowledge, and I will share my key learnings with you throughout this book.

How do I start my game plan early?

Your game plan began when you realized you could be a CEO. To ensure it has a strong start, you need to do three things:

1. Set high goals

2. Understand the value of your time

3. Use your time wisely.

✓ **You set a potential life goal – you said, "I am built to be CEO."**

By doing this, you are already ahead of many early- to mid-career professionals who have not invested enough time in defining their goals. Albert Einstein said, "If you want to live a happy life, tie it to a goal, not to people or things."
Don't be alarmed by the phrase "life goal," or commitment to it. Your goals can be adjusted, and you are not restricted to having one life goal, although I don't recommend too many.

You may even start thinking about your legacy. I encourage you to be on the lookout for a good one. My mentor Laura Furstenthal's legacy is to "Help create a generation of empowered, confident, and thoughtful women AND men who accomplish more than they ever thought they could." A female executive at AAA NCNU, Laura Zeigler, once told me: "I want to work for someone who I hired and trained." Both stand out to me because of their commitment to the betterment of themselves and others. They will be remembered for what they achieve and by others who achieved more because of them. I am possibly in the same place as you are. I am still in the process of crafting what my legacy could be, and that is okay.

How do I set my goals?

Your life goal also does not stand by itself – it is an amalgamation of aspirational goals and short-term goals. If you don't formulate your goals correctly, it will be much more challenging to accomplish them. Your short-term, aspirational and life goals must be, as many good managers would recommend, S.M.A.R.T:

- Specific. It is not enough to say, "I want to be successful." You must define what success means to you and pair it with one or more actions to indicate *how* you will achieve your specific goal.
- Measurable, then Motivational. Have a metric and a way of obtaining this metric that is associated with your goals. This is essentially a clear way to determine when you have achieved what you set out to do. Some self-help programs encourage the "M" in S.M.A.R.T. goals to stand for "motivational" instead of "measurable." Of course, motivation is always useful when you're setting a goal. However, creating a measurable goal will enable you to make it motivational.
- Achievable or attainable within your time frame, but flexible. Break a life or aspirational goal down into smaller building-blocks. It is better to take baby steps than one giant leap. When you encounter hurdles, adapt to your situation in order to move toward your bigger, more long-term goals. This might mean modifying your goals or even being willing to let go of a goal that is no longer meaningful to you and instead focusing on the bigger and more impactful objective.
- Realistic, but not negative. Your goals should be aimed based on what you yearn for rather than what you prefer to avoid. They should be compatible with your capabilities and talents. (Fortunately, becoming a CEO is in range for you.)
- Time-bound. Have a timeframe for achieving your goals, as well as a date where you will determine

the next step after achieving this goal. For example, you want to do your GMAT exam by January 20, and on that date you will begin preparing for your next exam.

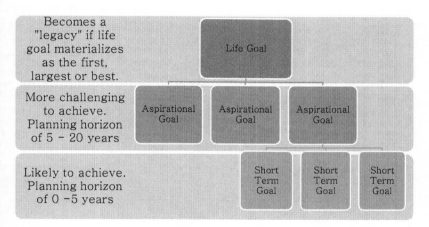

If you decide that becoming a CEO is your life or aspirational goal, you will need to define the aspirational or short-term goals that would help you achieve this bigger goal. For example, your aspirational goals could be:
- ✓ Obtain an MBA from a top-tier business school by a certain date
- ✓ Get promoted to manage a larger business within your company as a result of a project you are currently working on
- ✓ Gain Board experience in a certain industry by applying for a directorship, or engaging a recruiting company that will search for you

You could even benefit from breaking these goals down further. For example, to obtain an MBA, you first need to score high in the GMAT entry test, and your aim might be to take the test by a particular date.

How do I stick to my goals?

This will be a different experience for different people. Here are some ideas to motivate yourself to keep your goals promises intact.

First, you may have to **shift your perspective** on the importance of goals – by accepting that even though your goals may seen positive, achieving them might make you uncomfortable, and you will need to push yourself, and ignore those who don't believe in you, in order to attain them. Thomas Edison, who invented the light bulb, endured 10,000 attempts to create a light bulb. In response to his repeated failures he said, "I have not failed. I've just found 10,000 ways that won't work." Your career roadmap should and will be a challenge, not a cakewalk.

Once you've done this, you need to **digest your goals**. Research shows that people who write down their goals are significantly more likely to achieve those goals. This is linked to being able to find words to describe goals that appeal to you. Writing helps you remember and incorporate them into your life. It may also help to visualize what success looks like – using your mind's eye, envision yourself achieving that goal. Sports psychologists encourage their elite athletes to do something similar in order to make them feel motivated by their vision of success and familiar with the situation they are about to approach, so they are less intimidated by the journey. My mentor Jennifer Botterill, a four-time Olympic medalist, Harvard graduate and performance coach, encouraged me to do this, and I encourage you to use your mind's eye in this way as well.

Then, consider **reinforcing this plan** by using those around you and, potentially, a mentor or coach to hold yourself accountable. You do not necessarily need someone to help you reach every goal you have created, but the support that some provide can go a long way. If you've written down your goals, it will already be easier to share them with others.

The real secret to successfully achieving your goals is appreciating that our biggest goals will take longer to achieve, and that this makes them worth it. As you track your progress, **celebrate your small wins** and allow your brain to feel the dopamine rush of the building blocks of achievement as you reach a more elusive goal.

In the long term, successful habits equal success. **Rewarding your success** will give your brain and body an addiction to achieving the goals you set for yourself, and these habits will keep you going, even when the world seems like it wants you (like Thomas Edison!) to fail.

✓ You must value your time more than any other resource at your disposal.

Some people are born rich while others are born less fortunate. Some grew up with support from their families while others did not. Some have college degrees, others don't. Regardless of socio-economic status, everyone has the same number of hours in a day. Time is the lowest common denominator.

How do I calculate the value of my time?

The phrase "time is money" is accurate – time could produce value in the form of monetary gains. Every person who earns an income has some hourly rate of pay. Take a person's annual income and divide it by the number of hours they work in a given year.

- To determine the minimum, establish how much money you are making per year and divide it by 2,000, which

is about how many hours the average person works per year.
- To determine the maximum, consider how much you make for your most productive time – closing a deal, a speaking engagement, billable client time, etc.

Somewhere between those figures is the financial value of your time.

However, remember that time is significantly more valuable than that. A more accurate but frankly impossible (we cannot yet predict the future) way to calculate merely the financial value of money is to use *hindsight*. Some people decide how much money they would like to make in their lifetime, and then create goals for themselves by working their way backwards. Similarly, you could decide what level of success you would like to enjoy in the future and determine how your time should be used now to reach your goal. The value of your time now will be greater because of its growth potential and fundamental role in influencing your future. It is therefore difficult to assign a dollar value to one hour of your time now without fully understanding and calculating the current financial value as well as the value of its potential.

I am a firm believer that the value of your time cannot purely be a function of income. I believe it is also influenced by the activities you engage in, your productive capacity as a professional and the external environment.

The way you spend your time can influence your happiness and potential to succeed. Spending money can provide you with even more happiness than simply watching your savings or investment account balance go up. One study has shown that using money to buy free time, for example, paying to delegate household chores such as cleaning and cooking, is linked to greater life satisfaction.[xix]

Across the new world of business, where disruption is at every corner and "innovation" is the word of the day, CEOs and future CEOs must shift focus to the "money value of time" (MVT). Cutting-edge people and companies are rethinking the nature of their relationship with time. Occasionally, time is almost as measurable as money, but it is always more valuable. Businesses are using the scarcity of time as an opportunity to shape business models. Established companies offer to beat the time crunch – top investment banking and management consulting firms charge higher fees with the promise that they will deliver a high-quality product in a shorter period of time than their competitors. Often, this means analysts and associates are expected to work through the night to deliver the promises made by management. Businesses exploit time zones to maximize what the universe offers. Companies on the West Coast of the United States will hire a team on the East Coast and potentially in Asia to deliver projects overnight.

What is the MVT?

The Money Value of Time (MVT) is used to demonstrate the theoretical concept that there is a cost to participating in any activity. Economists call this "opportunity cost." While most people will calculate the value of their time using only their hourly wage or gross income, the money value of time is influenced by a number of other factors. The activities you engage in, your productive capacity as a professional and the external environment will all influence this calculation. While your final value may vary, one thing is clear: if you are aiming to be CEO, the present value of your time is greater than the same amount of time in the future.

Your value of time in the future may be higher – you have a higher income and you have fewer years left to enjoy it.

However, the MVT confirms a significantly higher opportunity cost early on in your career, when you are generally able to take more risks and use your time in a more flexible way.

How will the value of my time influence my early career?

Your three main personal resources – your income, your energy and your time – are finite. These resources are not in equal abundance through your life. In your *early career*, you have time and energy, but limited income. When you are *mid-career*, you enjoy a sustained level of high energy and generally a higher income, but are restricted on your disposable time. In your *late career*, closer to retirement, you regain time and have amassed money, but your energy levels are depleted and will continue to diminish.

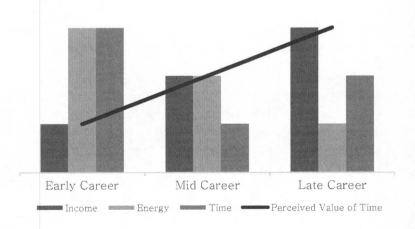

Our *perceived* value of time is often inversely tied to energy. Thus, our perceived value of time in the later part of our life, when we have limited energy, is at an all-time high. What we have failed to take into account is that time is a factor of both income and energy. Time well spent will grow financial assets and wealth, and your future energy levels, through a healthier lifestyle.

Our perceived value of time should be the highest in our early career. In fact, in our old age, we are likely to look back at our early career and possibly regret not taking enough risks or using the time we had in a different way.

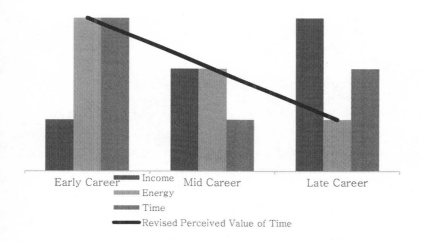

Early Career ▬ Income Mid Career   Late Career
▬ Energy
▬ Time
▬ Revised Perceived Value of Time

It is now more important that the time you have in your early career is spent well. This lesson came to me from a CEO I used to work closely with. He told me:

> You might be the youngest in the room, and the youngest to do many things. But at some point, you stop being the youngest. It will hit you when you realize you're the oldest. And you will look back and reflect on whether you could have achieved even more earlier on in your life, and regrets are expensive.

✓ **You should make life choices based on the value of your time.**

How might we maximize the value of time? How do we spend time and potentially money in order to make more time? How might we use this method to position ourselves to be future CEOs?

CEOs will tell you every minute counts, and this chapter outlines concepts, reasons and processes for maximizing the value of every minute.

1. **Spend time creating your goals and accomplishing them.**
2. **Spend time preparing yourself for your path to CEO.** The world we live in is generally male-dominated, with lingering biases against women in leadership. Additionally, the CEO position is a challenging one and demands certain personality traits and unmatched resilience.
3. **Spend time building your resume.** *Chapter 6: The Resume Builders* will focus on the basics and sweeteners you need to be a CEO.
4. **Spend time driving your agenda.** At work, proactively seek to build technical and communication skills, and executive support in advance of when you need it. Beyond work, understand the spider web of the industry you operate in and the financial ecosystem you are contributing to. Determine if you would make your future easier by devoting time to institutions and causes outside work or by investing in educational courses. *Chapter 7: The Agenda Drivers, Chapter 8: The Support Boosters* and *Chapter 9: The Cherry on Top* will dive deep into how to develop personality traits, communication skills and personal brand to drive your goals through your career.

5. **Spend time constantly improving yourself.** Allocate money to take vacations to recharge your body, your mind and your relationships. If you manage people, tell Team Members to question *your* decisions. Their advice will help you become more efficient.

At the same time, avoid making mistakes with your time in your early career.
The most painful ones I have witnessed are:

- Thinking you know it all. To build a successful career, you need to develop expertise in your field, but when you allow yourself to think you have to know everything and do everything, you are setting yourself up for failure.

- Thinking you don't need to put effort in. You may be extremely competent in what you do, but if you don't have any leadership coaching, mentoring or guidance, you cannot expect that what got you to your position will keep you there. If you plan to be a future CEO, you need to be constantly honing your skills.

- Being easily distracted. This can be by job titles, in your early career, versus the skills the job offers; or new, shiny projects with limited upward potential; or even spending excessive amounts of time on social media – that time adds up and it could have been put to better use.

- Putting your career success before your family and health. You might end up with nothing. My mother told me once, "Some people are so poor that they only have money." That statement has become imprinted on my mind, and I hope it will be on yours too.

- Burning bridges. This may be the biggest mistake of all. It is tempting to do because you assume you are moving on and do not need to look back, or you feel wronged and you want some type of revenge. But the short-term satisfaction of this can cost you in reputation. There is a good chance you will run into some of these people again, and your interactions could be awkward. If your actions have closed doors, it could be potentially harmful to your future career.

Your early career rests on your ability to set goals and value your time. How you think about valuing your time will determine how you spend it.

Time is where you bleed creative energy; time is when your motivation grows or dies. We live in a world where Netflix allows us less than 15 seconds to decide whether we are going to do anything productive with our day. I believe our perceived value of time over our lifetime is flawed. It might even be a limiting factor in encouraging early-career future CEOs to invest time now to grow.

Chapter 3
The Force Fields in your Environment

Before you dive into constructing your path(s) to become CEO, it is worth knowing that today's society may have an unconscious bias against women in business leadership positions. Here are a few broad strokes:

- *The words that make up CEO – "chief," "executive" and "officer" – have gendered connotations.* In English, all three of those words are linked to men. Think about it. Do not let this stop you.

- *The history of the CEO role is male-dominated.* The term "chief executive officer" is thought to have originated in 1917, roughly the time when Henry Ford established the modern managerial form of corporate business, with people hired to run functions and business units.[xx] In the mid-20th century, the quintessential CEO was a founder of a new industry, like advanced technology, finance, fast food, air transportation, and entertainment. The role was filled with men – Bill Allen (Boeing), Ray Kroc (McDonald's), Howard Clark (American Express), Walt Disney (Walt Disney Company), Juan Trippe (Pan Am) and Thomas Watson Jr. (IBM). In 1955, another man – Edgar P. Smith coined the concept of The Fortune 500.

Granted, there were women who managed their own companies, such as Anna Bissell who inherited the Bissell company, known for inventing and patenting an innovative carpet sweeper after her husband's death in 1889. Katharine Graham, America's first female

Fortune 500 CEO in 1972, took over The Washington Post after her husband's death. These women, however, hardly shared the spotlight that history gave to businessmen and their marvelous inventions. Do not let this stop you.

- *Even today's society is likely to pin men over women to leadership positions.* In an experiment featured in the New York Times, participants were asked to call into a monthly sales team meeting of a fictional company, during which they would hear from either an Eric or an Erica. Later, they were asked to rate the speaker on the degree to which he or she had "exhibited leadership," "influenced the team" or "assumed a leadership role." The Erics were ranked higher. The Ericas did not receive a boost in ratings from sharing ideas even though they were exactly the same as the Erics.[xxi] Do not let this stop you.

Even the thing commonly seen as a weakness of women, menstruation, might not be. It might actually be to our advantage. Studies show that pre-menopausal women may possess a keener sense of focus than men and post-menopausal women. The Stroop Test measures a person's selective attention capacity and skills, as well as their processing speed ability. Women under 60 performed far better than men, suggesting they have better multi-tasking abilities. The front runner in explaining these results is that estrogen can reshape neural networks and perhaps improve function in the prefrontal cortex. In the environment we live in today, height and physical strength are not as important. Women are not at a biochemical disadvantage: we could actually be at an advantage.

So, what could be reinforcing biases against women?

It is an invisible force field. You interact with it often and willingly. It reflects our biases and reinforces them, and may even be causing them. We have allowed it to become our reality. I spy with my little eye, something that begins with "H," and ends in "ollywood."

In Hollywood, women are not seen.

The Bechdel test asks whether a work of fiction features at least two women who talk to each other about something other than a man. The test is used as an indicator for the active presence of women in films and other fiction, and to call attention to gender inequality in fiction.

Only half of all films pass this test.[xxii] The Bechdel test should not be a hard test to pass.

There is an alarming underrepresentation of women in front of the camera:

- There were on average 2.3 male characters for every woman, with no meaningful change from 2007 to 2016. [xxiii]

- Crowd shots in general have an average of only 17% women.[xxiv] This is a ratio that has not changed since 1946.

- Of the top 100 films of 2016 (determined by the list of the 100 top fictional films on Box Office Mojo), only 34 had a woman lead – eight had a woman lead over the age of 45, and just three had a lead or co-lead from an underrepresented racial group.

There is also an alarming underrepresentation of diversity behind the camera:

- According to the study mentioned in the previous point, only 20.7% of producers are women, 13.2% are writers, 4.2% are directors and just 1.7% are composers.

- Across 1,006 directors of the 900 films analyzed by a study, 53 were Black men, three were Black women, and two were Asian women. [xxv]

Women are barely seen at the top of the business world as well – they make up fewer than 5% of Fortune 500 CEOs. With fewer women in senior positions, younger women have access to fewer mentors. More notably, the image of the North American moose, sitting in the seat of the CEO, becomes more prevalent and, at times, more discouraging for young women who are aiming for the CEO position but look different.

In Hollywood, women are not heard.
An in-depth study of Hollywood screenplays found that, across thousands of films, it was hard to find a subset that did not over-index male. What makes this especially harmful is that women are the biggest consumers of movies: women purchase *more than half* of all movie tickets sold each year.[xxvi]

- *Number of speaking parts* – Only 18% of films have women as two of the top three speaking parts (a scenario that male actors go into 82% of the time).[xxvii]
- *Ratio of speaking parts by gender* – For every woman who speaks even in films, there are around three male speaking characters. In *Star Wars: The Force Awakens*, 78% of the dialogue was spoken by men and some minor male roles had more lines than the main female character, Rey. Even more alarmingly, this film had the highest percentage of dialogue spoken by women of all Star Wars movies. In the original movie,

Episode IV, only 6% of the dialogue was spoken by women.

- *Top Speaking Parts* – Research has found that females comprised only 12% of protagonists in the top-grossing films of 2014. In secondary roles, females are also underrepresented, comprising 29% of major characters and 30% of all speaking characters.

In the business world, where women make up only 5% of Fortune 500 CEOs, they may be lacking a voice in the room. This could impact decisions that impact women, like what benefits women receive in the workplace or, in situations that pertain to harassment, what the outcome for the perpetrator is and what support the victim gets.

Sheryl Sandberg's book, *Lean In*, reveals how women are not heard in the workplace. The one positive is that the Fortune 500 companies are appointing more women to Boards of Directors seats than ever before. While it's not gender parity, women accounted for 38.3% of all newly named Board Directors of Fortune 500 companies in 2017, according to executive search firm Heidrick & Struggles. In 2019, California became the first state to require publicly held corporations headquartered in the state to include women on their boards. Having women on Boards is a start to giving women a voice at the top.

You may have been impacted since before you remember.
We have likely been conditioned to accept these gender discrepancies since we were young.

When I re-watched, in my mid-20's, the Disney princess movies I thoroughly enjoyed in my childhood, I was reminded how the roles played by females often depended on assistance from men. The princess's father controls the princess. The princess is then saved by a prince, like in

The Little Mermaid, Cinderella and Sleeping Beauty. For example, Lady in Lady and the Tramp is helpless and remains in a supporting role, only to accept the responsibilities of motherhood in the end. Perhaps we can learn from Jasmine, who charts her own destiny. She dislikes her pampered life as the Sultan's daughter, disguises herself as a peasant to escape the palace and experience the life of a regular citizen. She rejects princes to marry Aladdin for love.

Additionally, the other women in the film generally encourage and are responsible for adversity. Snow White's step-mother tries to kill her with a poison apple. Queen Maleficent put Princess Aurora in a coma, and then transformed into a fire-breathing dragon to ensure she stayed in the coma.

More notably, I noticed that female characters in these movies hardly spoke. I found a study, published by *The Washington Post*, by linguists Carmen Fought and Karen Eisenhauer, that analyzed dialogue in Disney princess movies from 1989 to 1999, also known as Disney's "Renaissance" era.[xxviii] It found that men spoke 71% of the time in Beauty and the Beast (1991) and 76% of the time in Pocahontas (1995).[xxix]

With time, Disney gave female characters more speaking time and roles. Disney's Tangled (2010) had female characters speak 52% of the lines, and Disney's Brave (2012), where men spoke 26% of the dialogue, boasted significant improvements from the princess films released in the 20th century. In the movie Wreck-It Ralph 2: Ralph Breaks the Internet (2018), Disney even acknowledged its failure to empower women. In one scene, the collection of Disney princesses – Cinderella, Jasmine, Belle, Tiana, Pocahontas – say that in order to be one of them, "people assume all your problems get solved because a big, strong man showed up."

As a huge fan of Disney movies when I was young, I was influenced by the princesses in these films. When I was younger, I saw these women as my idols. Like Ariel, I allowed older men to control my opinions, instead of being defiant and standing up for what I believed was true. I prioritized my relationships with men over how I wanted to spend my time and what my mental health was asking for.

The products of Hollywood reflect the notion that women are not seen or heard in our societal and cultural environment. As society continues to passively accept and absorb gender discrepancies in movies, the absence of the female voice and face becomes normal in other films we watch and possibly even in our workplaces. This becomes a real problem.

The Takeaways: Real Lessons From La-La Land

While women make up a larger share of movie audiences in the US than men, and female-led movies have a stronger return-on-investment than male-led movies, their voices and faces are underrepresented in the film industry.[xxx]

Similarly, and as I highlighted in the *Introduction* of this book, S&P 500 businesses now run by women are outperforming those run by their male counterparts. Despite this, women are severely underrepresented in the CEO position.

There are a number of lessons that the business world can take away from the film industry in order for you to build an environment where you can succeed without invisible force fields.

The world operates from a male perspective.
Most stories are told specifically *from* a male perspective *for* a male perspective. According to an interview piece,

Screenwriter Susannah Grant stated that the industry views "chick flicks," typically aimed at women, as dead animals at the box office. Chick flicks, typically considered to be aimed at women, should be absolute hits, primarily because more than half of the movie-goers are female. Some believe they're objectively bad. But most chick flicks are directed by males, for females. So, if the characters and plot do not seem real, it is likely because they are borne from a male perspective.

The business world operates this way as well. I once attended a small group meeting at a product marketing conference in Silicon Valley. The all-day event was filled with representatives from the most forward-looking companies in the technology and business worlds. The representation of females to males was roughly equal. Despite this, a panel of four people continued to refer to hypothetical business leaders as "he." Not once was that CEO or Head of Product a "she," even when the question was asked by a female and answered by a female panelist. This not only perpetuates a belief in a reality where men hold executive roles for men, but for women as well. And, congruently, we see fewer females rise to the top.

Sexist stereotypes exist.
A recent survey by Advertising Women of New York (AWNY) of professional men and women in several communications fields found some revealing differences in current perceptions. More than half of the women surveyed said that the "old boys" network and sexist attitudes inhibited their career growth. The men – 80% of them – did not see the issue of sexism; they believed women have equal opportunities in the areas of responsibility, promotion and salary.

As much as movies may reflect the world we live in, they may also be taken by their audience as what is expected of the world. One of my mentors, Patti Lee, shared a story with me that depicts this. When she was searching for job opportunities as a television reporter, she was told by one company that they "already had an Asian representative," and therefore she was not needed.

The business world operates this way as well. In 2017, the New York Times released a powerful piece featuring real people recounting real stories in the workplace. The first story involved a male colleague saying to a female colleague, "I'm sure you know a lot about cleaning," and the people around them had the audacity to chuckle. Each story seemed more discriminatory than the previous one. A heated phone conversation between a male and female lawyer led to the male lawyer telling his counterpart take a pill for menstrual cramps and hanging up the phone.

This issue is even prevalent in the world of science. A study conducted by the L'Oréal Foundation found that 67% of Europeans think that women do not possess the required skill set in order to achieve high-level scientific positions. The figure is 64% in the UK. In China, 93% believe that women are not built to be scientists.

By allowing gender-based stereotyping to persist, however, we risk losing opportunities that could strengthen and accelerate the path of women to CEO. Backgrounds in STEM (Science, Technology, Engineering, Mathematics), business and finance have proven to be launch-pads for female CEOs. According to a study conducted by the Harvard Business Review on 57 female CEOs, 40% of the female CEOs started out with some technical expertise in STEM. Close to 20% started with a background in business, finance, or economics. None of these women started in Human Resources, a field where women are disproportionately represented.[xxxi]

The mother of one of my mentors, Laura Furstenthal, was one of the early woman math majors at UC Berkeley. However, after graduating, she got paid half of what men did in the same scientific jobs and eventually quit to raise her kids, as was expected of her. Imagine if it was commonplace to see women succeed in these positions.

On your journey to CEO, do not let these stereotypes limit you; acknowledge that they exist, and fight them by defying them.

Women encounter unsavory behavior too often.

In spite of the #MeToo movement in Hollywood and the sexual harassment headlines that stained Uber, Fox News and other conglomerates, sexual harassment remains embedded in organizational culture and American society. According to an *LA Times* story, women in entertainment are more vulnerable to sexual harassment than women in other industries.[xxxii] A study by the Advertising Women of New York (AWNY) indicated that 35% of the professional women polled had some personal experience with sexual harassment, though most of them did not officially report it.

This is rampant in the business world as well, despite 98% of organizations in the United States have a sexual harassment policy. We still see both men and women shame other women for "making noise," or encouraging sexually harassed women to quit their jobs without considering that perhaps the perpetrators instead of their targets should exit. This has material impacts on how harassment is judged. In the Fox News suit, the alleged offenders received more robust settlements than the targets.[xxxiii]

On your journey to CEO, never tolerate abuse in any capacity, always support the women around you and have a good lawyer on speed dial.

You may be offered less money than your male counterparts.

The dragon in Disney's animated film Mulan had more speaking time than the main character – Mulan. These are movies that feature strong female roles in them, and still men spoke significantly more and received higher compensation. The same thing applies to the actors. Although Julia Roberts is acclaimed as one of the elite top ten stars in terms of box-office, salary and power, women receive only a third of all movie and TV roles, and earn less than male actors in all age categories except those in their twenties. Women over 40 get about 9% of parts, while men over 40 get 27%, according to an essay about women in film by Douglas Eby.[xxxiv] In executive positions at major studios there are still four times as many men as women.

Oscar-winner Emma Stone, the world's highest-paid actress, earned $26 million in 2017, which amounted to less than half the amount the highest-paid actor made: action star Mark Wahlberg, who topped the men's ranking, earned $68 million. The Netflix show "The Crown" acknowledged that Claire Foy, who played the main character Queen Elizabeth II, received less compensation than her co-star Matt Smith, who played the queen's husband, Prince Philip.

As Elaine Goldsmith-Thomas (Julia Roberts's agent) has said, "I don't know why people think the entertainment business is different than any other. Maybe the glass ceiling has been raised a bit. But certainly, when a woman hits her head on it, she can look up and see men's loafers." [xxxv]

In the business world, this is certainly true as well. Women are not paid the same as men for their time, and this may not be fixed for decades. According to the Institute for Women's Policy Research, women will need to *wait* until at least 2059, based on current trends, to receive equal pay. The majority of people alive today are unlikely to live long enough to see this happen. This could include you.

Similar to the sluggish pace at which the number of female Fortune 500 CEOs has grown, the wage gap has experienced only incremental improvements since the Equal Pay Act was signed in 1963. In 1963, women who worked full-time, year-round, for only 59 cents on average for every dollar earned by men. In 2010, women earned only 77 cents to men's dollar. The wage gap has narrowed by less than half a cent per year. Moreover, women work on average 50 minutes longer a day and have a much slimmer chance of reaching senior roles.[xxxvi]

■Paid Work (Hours)　■Unpaid Work (Hours)

Additionally, over the past 40 years, the real median earnings of women have fallen short by an estimated $700,000 to $2 million. Over a lifetime (47 years of full-time work) this gap amounts to a loss in wages for a woman of $700,000 for a high school graduate, $1.2 million for a college graduate and $2 million for a professional school graduate.[xxxvii]

In April 2019, TIME revealed that a woman would have to work over three months more in order to make what her male counterpart did per year for the same full time work.

In other words, this equates to about $900 billion in annual lost earnings for women holding full-time jobs in 2018.[xxxviii]

Let that sink in, for you as well as the women around you who choose to work.

Year of Wage-Gap Close by State

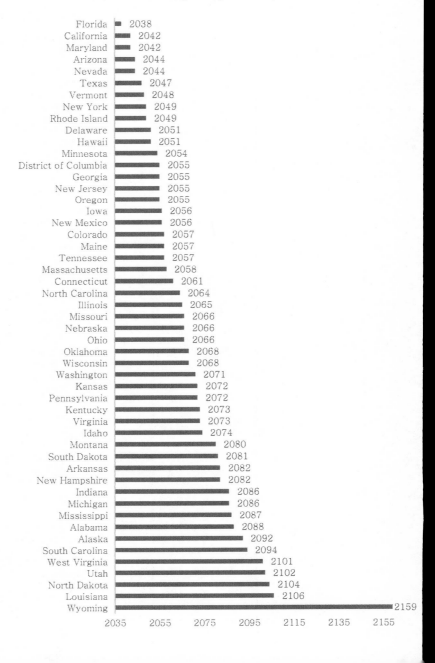

Although these realities may seem out of your control, they do not need to be. When Billie Jean King won the United States Open singles tennis title in 1972, her reward was a meager $10,000. Ilie Năstase, her male counterpart, won $25,000. Billie Jean took matters into her own hands and used her skills, experience, connections and name in the tennis industry to fight for equal rights. And she won. By 1973, men and women received the same prizes at the U.S. Open (although not all tennis tournaments – there is still more work to do).

As assistant secretary of labor and director of the Women's Bureau during the Kennedy administration, Esther Peterson spearheaded the campaign to authorize the 1963 Equal Pay Act. Esther Peterson and other activists put pressure on President Kennedy and Congress to make the law. More recently, in 2018, Iceland made it illegal to pay women less than men. This law impacted over 300,000 Icelandic citizens. To extend this to over 300 million American citizens, we need to push for an end to mandatory arbitration as a condition of employment. This would allow women, and men, to win back their constitutional rights to a trial by a jury of their peers. To march towards equal pay, our society needs transparency, as well as legitimate legal scrutiny.

On your journey to CEO, do not accept anything less than equal; do not stop fighting for what you are worth.

The film industry hardly empathizes with your personal schedule.

A Senior Vice President at Universal Pictures and President of Women in Film (Los Angeles), among a number of other creative and leadership roles, Hollace Davids has admitted to experiencing conflicts between career and personal priorities. Davids has talked about the Hollywood industry – the business side of movie-making:

> I've always had to battle the feeling that I should be home when I'm at work and vice versa··· It's really helped that my husband works at home and is a supportive partner. He's the one who'd take the kids to the dentist, and during spring break, which is Academy Awards time, he'd take the kids on a vacation. ... If they tell you that you can have it all, don't believe it. You can do many things, but not without compromise. There just isn't enough time in the day to do everything 100%. I've tried not to get swept up in putting value on the wrong things – the big house, the new car. A good family life is more important than a new car.[xxxix]

This is true in the business world as well. In a study by Furman University's Christin Munsch, the reactions that men and women receive when requesting flexible work requests are different, and were favorable to men. In comparing the transcripts and the reactions of over 600 working-age individuals, the study found that when male employees requested flexible schedules to accommodate childcare requests, close to 70% of participants were either likely or very likely to allow the request, as opposed to only 57% allowing the request for females. The participants also evaluated men as more committed and likeable than women.[xl]

I, for example, worked at a fairly progressive large organization in Northern California that boasted a majority-female executive team. Some had tenure at the company and some were newer. What stood out to me was the fact that half did not have children. These women were extremely successful and could have undoubtedly juggled

58

a successful career and having 50 children, if they sought to do so. However, given the societal biases against women who choose to juggle career and family life, I could not help but wonder whether these impressive women had to consider choosing between an accelerated, successful career or having children and potentially risking their careers twenty years ago. I sure hope not, but this bias certainly exists for a number of women across the globe.

You may not have the support network you need.
Talent agencies in Hollywood could be more influential than film studios in controlling the top of the funnel and producing projects. The Chairman of ICM (International Creative Management – an organization dedicated to the representation of artists, content creators, authors, etc.) Jeff Berg stated, "Part of the old boy network has been stripped away. But the fact remains that the three major agencies are operated by men. Many more women have entered the ranks; but it goes beyond numbers to attitudes."

This is true in the business world, especially in the tech-industry. Despite its liberal nature – Tesla is attempting to save the world with electric vehicles, Uber aims to change global mobility, Google and Facebook continue to be at the forefront of human connectivity – tech still operates as an old boys' club to an extent.
An industry-wide survey in 2017, conducted in Silicon Valley on more than 200 women in tech with at least 10 years of experience, found that 60% of the women had experienced "unwanted sexual advances," 87% reported that they had received "demeaning comments from male colleagues," and 75% said they had been (illegally) asked about their marital status, children and/or family life in job interviews.

Even the boards of these "liberal" technology companies skew male. Google had three women out of 12 board members, Apple had two out of eight, and Uber had one in seven (Arianna Huffington, who famously joined the board) in 2017.[xli]

On your journey to CEO, invest time, effort and money in finding and refining your support structure. Investing in building your network is not the same as being selfish, and it hardly goes to waste. This is the focus and highlight of Chapter 8: The Support Boosters.

What impact will this have on me and my journey? How do I build an environment I can thrive in?

If you are able to understand the force fields as they pertain to your journey to CEO, you are halfway there. Your efforts to combat force fields could reduce the friction on your path and on the paths of other young women who aspire to be CEO someday soon.

One important lesson is that women in leadership positions seem to help more women move into leadership positions. In the film industry, there is a positive correlation between women in decision-making positions and the number of women being seen and heard on screen. When female writers and directors were women, 39% of protagonists in films were women, compared to 4% when the filmmaker was a man.[xlii] This means that movies written or directed by a female are ten times more likely to feature a woman as the main character.

It is no wonder there is such a gender discrepancy in the film industry – women have written only about 17% of all the screenplays produced in the 21st century so far.

In the business world, this could also be true. Using this logic, the way to truly build an environment that you will succeed in will require more women in leadership positions.

Empowered women become role models when they empower other women. It is as simple as that. You will empower other women when you are empowered too.

Empowered women remind others that gender discrepancies should be unacceptable. In Reese Witherspoon's speech at *Glamor* 2015's Woman of the Year event, she surfaced the five words that women consistently say in the movies, but never in real life – "What do we do now?" It served as a call to action for better understanding and more representation of women as film writers.

Empowered women will break down gender barriers. Paramount CEO Sherry Lansing once stated, "When I first got the job at Fox, a bunch of women took me out and said, 'You have to succeed, or you'll let us women down.' Then one woman said, 'Wait a minute, men have been failing at this job for years!'"[xliii] As the President of production at 20th Century Fox, she was the first woman to head a Hollywood movie studio, and a trailblazer.

Empowered women pave the way for change. Director Martha Coolidge notes that when she applied to film school, she was told that as a woman she just could not be a director. She didn't accept that attitude. She said, "It didn't occur to me that I couldn't do it. Gender is not a demarcation of what one can or cannot do."

The statistics tell a sobering story of women in television and movies and prove even more the importance of sharing stories of successful, strong and talented women as part of our nation's narrative. Unsurprisingly, the gender discrepancies in the business world bear a stark resemblance to those plaguing the film industry.

Gender biases stretch across industries. They impact women across age groups, race, socio-economic statuses and career paths. In Hollywood, this issue seems to be more controllable when women assume leadership positions, and then enable other women to be seen and heard. So naturally, the most apparent learning to me is that we need more female CEOs, pronto.

Chapter 4
The Types & Traits of CEOs

Personality types track back all the way to Ancient Greece. Hippocrates hypothesized two poles on which temperament could vary, hot vs. cold and moist vs. dry, to form four possible combinations, or "humors," to describe different personalities. Plato classified personalities into artistic, sensible, intuitive and reasoning. His student, Aristotle, proposed a similar set of factors that could explain personality: iconic (or artistic), pistic (or common sense), noetic (intuition) and dianoetic (or logic).

The good news is that you do not need to fit into a particular personality type to be a future CEO. In fact, the notion of being identified by merely personality type is going out of style, according to multiple publications of *The Journal of Psychological Type*. Humans are complex beings, governed by changing internal and external environmental complicators that make it almost impossible to proclaim, with 100% certainty, that each has one type of personality.

This chapter will, instead, focus on the *traits* that you will need to develop and exhibit to become a successful CEO, and how to acquire these traits on your path to the top.

Are personality test results useless?

They are not *completely* useless. The most common personality tests used by the corporate world – DISC, Enneagram, Dark Triad and the Meyers Briggs – are restrictive and mostly diagnostic because they fit people

63

into one particular "type," and do not provide recommendations for developing favorable traits. Nevertheless, they cultivate a basic sense of self-awareness that could serve as a first step in fostering the traits you need. If you have taken any of the four most common corporate tests, take them with a grain of salt.

Adapting the DISC Personality Test. This test is used to make communication more effective by helping participants understand how one person would be likely to react in a specific team, management, or leadership situation, given their DISC style. The tool's origins date back to the early 1920s. It was developed by William Marston, who was not only a lawyer and a psychologist, but also the producer of the first functional lie detector polygraph and the creator of the *Wonder Woman* comic. DISC stands for:

- Dominance (D) – Dominant, or Visionary people are classic leaders with a vision for change who call others to follow and help. Consider Marie Curie and Golda Meir.
- Inducement or Influence (I) – Influencers, that is, peacemakers who transform not through their own agenda, but through bringing others together. Consider Jane Goodall and several winners of the Nobel Peace Prize.
- Submission or Steadiness (S) – Steady leaders in challenging times lead the country or the company in the face of adversity. Consider Margaret Thatcher.
- Compliance or Conscientiousness (C) – Cooperative people who are problem solvers, working well with others. Consider former First Lady of the United States and Secretary of State Hillary Rodham Clinton.

Marston's work has been further developed over time, and now proposes four general orientations for judging the effectiveness of your communication skills in the workplace: *Outgoing* (Dominance and Influence), *People* (Influence and Steadiness), *Reserved* (Steadiness and Compliance) and *Task* (Compliance and Dominance).

If you have taken this test, use your results to become more aware of your communication style. Understand what you have and do not have yet. Ask yourself, "What personality traits have led to me falling into a DISC type like Outgoing or Reserved?" and "What traits do I need to develop?" And read on – this chapter will outline what traits you will need to become a CEO in the future.

Adapting the Enneagram Assessment. This test is a description of the human psyche, which is principally understood and taught as a typology of nine interconnected personality types: reformer, helper, achiever, individualist, investigator, loyalist, enthusiast, challenger and peacemaker. Each gifts a sense of purpose to the test taker.

If you have taken this test, ask yourself, "What do I do for others and what don't I do?" Use the CEO traits highlighted later in this chapter to identify what you need to begin nurturing. For example, I fall into the "Achiever" type and realize I am lacking all the CEO traits built within the other types that make them successful.

Adapting the Dark Triad Personality Test. This test outlines three traits that all have a somewhat malicious subtext: Machiavellianism (a manipulative attitude), narcissism (excessive self-love) and psychopathy (lack of empathy). In general, we tend to avoid seeing the worst characteristics about ourselves. When I took this test, I was bucketed into Machiavellianism, which essentially warned me that I had a manipulative attitude. Note that personality tests can imply binaries, which are usually not the case; for example, I might exhibit a manipulative attitude more than the other two dark qualities but this behavior might be more circumstantial than universal. Nevertheless, I took this result as a warning signal, and forced myself to be more cognizant about the way I request what I need. For example, I now intentionally ask more questions to the person I am requesting something from rather than demanding what I need.

This test allows corporations to pre-determine and have foresight into the "worst" traits about their employees, and gives employees the chance to course-correct early. If you have taken this test, use these results, with the content discussed later in this chapter, to understand what traits could build and break you on your path to CEO.

Adapting the Meyers Briggs Type Indicator (MBTI). Created by Katharine Cook Briggs and her daughter Isabel Briggs Myers, this indicator stemmed from Carl Jung's theory that overarching "types" of personalities can be discerned from dichotomous variables. This personality test is, by far, the most popular business personality test. Today, about 80% of Fortune 500 companies use it to analyze the personalities of employees, in an effort to put them in the right roles and help them succeed. Most entrepreneurs and business owners have taken a Myers-Briggs personality test at some point. If you ask around, you will immediately hear someone rattle off a string of letters. It is an introspective self-report questionnaire, that uses four situations in, for example, the workplace:

- **Favorite world:** Do you prefer to focus on the outer world or on your own inner world? This is called Extraversion (E) or Introversion (I).
- **Information:** Do you prefer to focus on the basic information you take in or do you prefer to interpret and add meaning? This is called Sensing (S) or Intuition (N). I have a fun wordplay here. Take the word "investor," a term used to describe someone who commits an existing resource for growth based on the external environment. If you switch out the "s" for "n," you get "inventor" – someone who grows ideas that do not already exist. This is how I differentiate these two variables.
- **Decisions:** When making decisions, do you prefer to first look at logic and consistency or first look at the people and special circumstances? This is called Thinking (T) or Feeling (F). According to the Statistic Brain Research Institute (SBRI), 75.5% of women are Feelers and 56.5% of men are Thinkers.[xliv] Additionally, women with an MBTI preference for Thinking (versus Feeling) are more likely to be called "aggressive" – I have experienced this first-hand![xlv]
- **Structure:** In dealing with the outside world, do you prefer to get things decided or do you prefer to stay open to new information and options? This is called Judging (J) or Perceiving (P).

Testing to be a certain type of person will not make you a CEO. Like DISC, Enneagram and Dark Triad, you can use your Meyers Briggs test results to identify your strengths. In this case, the sixteen personality types can be categorized by their strengths, which can be used to recommend optimal career path or industry for your type.

- **Pragmatists** (ESTJ, ISTJ, ESTP) love their work when they can use logical systems to produce tangible benefits.
- **Caretakers** (ESFJ, ISFJ, ESFP, ISFP) love their work when they can do practical things to help other people.
- **Theorists** (ENTJ, INTJ, ENTP, INTP) love their work when they can come up with innovative new ideas and inventions.
- **Empaths** (ENFJ, INFJ, ENFP, INFP) love their work when they can improve people's lives and make the world a more beautiful place.

You will find the most value, however, in understanding the *traits* that make "CEO Types" – commonly the category given to ENTJs, ESTJs, ENTPs, INTJs and ISTJs.

They are curious. ISTJs have a preference for strong evidence and solid justification, which often leads them to actively investigate the underlying logic of everything. As the architects of the group, INTJs revel in pushing the boundaries of what is possible. ENTPs enjoy abstractions and new knowledge.

They are creative. ENTPs are labeled "inventors" and appreciate novel and transformative ideas. INTJs, who often internalize their visions and the iterative steps to create them, produce ideas that have yet to be socialized. A 2004 British study determined that creativity was the single most critical and prevalent trait associated with entrepreneurship. It is so key, in fact, that in one study undergraduate students' divergent thinking and creativity successfully predicted their entrepreneurial intentions.[xlvi]

They take responsibility. ESTJs respect authority and discipline and, as a result, will hold themselves accountable (sometimes to a flaw). ENTJs welcome obstacles as a challenge. INTJs feel personally responsible for implementing their ideas. Modern psychologists call this mindset "internal locus of control," and it repeatedly makes entrepreneurial must-have lists. People with an internal locus of control believe that they are in control of their destiny. In fact, many studies consistently and convincingly find positive correlations between internal locus of control, business success and even career satisfaction.

They are decisive. ISTJs build step-by-step logical processes to achieving goals with minimal distractions. ESTJs implement decisions rapidly and methodically. INTJs and ENTJs create strategic action plans and are deeply satisfied when their tactics are successful. A 2004 U.S. study found a negative relationship between an entrepreneur's openness and long-term venture survival, while extraversion, emotional stability, and agreeableness were unrelated to long-term venture survival.[xlvii]

So, while personality test results will not automatically guarantee that you will become a CEO in the future, they will tell you what you over-index in, and what you might be missing. Taking these tests is a roundabout way of approaching personal and leadership development. Remember – take personality tests like the Meyers-Briggs with a grain of salt. The personality traits discussed in detail, in the next section, will outline what traits make successful CEOs, although the ENTJ has a preference for developing a number of these naturally.

If you intend to use a tool or test to better understand your existing personality and develop the characteristics that would propel you to the C-Suite, I recommend focusing on *traits, not types*. Traits are indicators, not measurements, and can be used to heighten self-awareness and promote self-development.

CEO Traits

The journey to becoming a CEO requires hard work to develop specific personality traits. You need to:

1. **Accelerate** your growth opportunities, to climb that ladder. This requires drive, curiosity, humility and adaptability.

2. **Align** your personal goals with your professional goals, to create a force in a favorable direction. This requires purpose, passion and engagement.

3. **Exhibit** the traits that would make a CEO successful in her role. This requires creativity, grit, decisiveness and emotional intelligence.

Here is the good news: all of these personality traits can be absorbed, learned and incorporated into your leadership journey. The most effective way to incorporate the traits that make a successful CEO and build future CEOs is to start practicing these skills now.

1. Traits that accelerate growth opportunities.

Continue to ask yourself, "To what extent do I possess this trait?" And "What can I do to develop it?" Some of these recommended actions will not deliver instantly. The earlier you begin to develop these traits in your career, the better.

Drive – _a self-motivational trait pushing you to excel regardless of the resources and opportunities you have._

- **Start with setting ambitious, future-focused goals:** Best-in-class leaders are always looking toward the future, setting ambitious goals. CEOs take initiative, are quicker to capitalize on opportunities and are more likely to take high-level risks than their other executive counterparts. Their intensity and passion for growth and development makes them charismatic and persuasive. You can start now, by setting higher goals.
- **Aim for a track record of high performance:** Potential CEOs, like other standout employees within a company's leadership pipeline, are characterized not only by their excellent performance track records, but their desire to take the reins on more challenging leadership positions. A good indicator of future success in a challenging role, like CEO, is past success. If you have not exhibited high performance or high potential yet, you can simply decide to change your trajectory, mindset and behavior to excel. It is never too late.
- **Reliably deliver results:** The ability to reliably produce results was the most powerful of CEO behaviors, according to a Harvard Business Review study. In their sample, CEO candidates who scored high on reliability were twice as likely to be picked for the role and 15 times more likely to succeed in it.[xlviii] Boards and investors look for consistency, and employees trust predictable leaders. Be sure to set clear goals for yourself, and share them with those who will be holding you accountable for reaching them (like your team, peers, manager and manager once removed); once you reach your goals, communicate this to these stakeholders to build your equity as a reliable worker.

- **Build strong relationships**. The ability to form deep relationships could make or break your path to being a CEO. Chapter 7 and 8 will dive deep into what it takes to build strong relationships and what you do should do with them. Relationships create loyalty and an image for the CEO and the company. Positive relationships also create good word-of-mouth feedback, and while your business may not run solely on that type of marketing, it can be helpful. Start by developing connections by investing heavily in your own emotional and social intelligence – solicit feedback about how others perceive you, learn from your limitations and engage actively with your employees and teams.

I have followed the four-point structure above to build my drive to overcome adversity during different life stages. For example, my parents did not go to college and were not equipped to assist me during the college application process. But I had my eyes set on the Ivy League. A few years later, I was applying for jobs during my senior year of college, and faced difficulty as an international student who did not have permission to stay and work in the United States. But I had my eyes set on a stable job in the U.S.

Drive, Curiosity, Humility, Adaptability.

Curiosity – *an introspective trait that allows you to actively yearn for more than what you have been offered.*

- **Live at your growth edge.** My grandmother always said, "Smart kids have long tongues" – that smart kids "talk back," and always ask "why." The smartest CEOs are vulnerable, open to hearing what they lack knowledge in, and are continuously engaged in learning new things. A key way to enable this trait is knowing what you do not know yet, and investing in bridging that gap. Avoid pretending to have all the answers – curious questioning is critical to accelerate your career growth. Be willing to learn everything about a business and industry. While you do not need to be the "expert" in all facets of the company, it is important to possess more than a passing knowledge of every department and operation, if you want to be the CEO. This helps in making key decisions and crafting a dynamic, all-encompassing vision of growth that integrates different functions into a cohesive whole.

- **Encourage yourself through realistic optimism:** Find a balance between daydreaming about ideas and the blunt practicalities of everyday life. The best CEOs are able to remain curious and grounded simultaneously. They are extremely aware of the pieces on the chessboard, and how certain moves will affect the position of the company, but they are also willing to consider unconventional solutions. Future CEOs should be confident, but not arrogant about their skills, and should remain aware of and confront challenges while still striving to reach ambitious goals.

Drive, Curiosity, **Humility**, Adaptability.

Humility – another introspective trait that allows you to ground yourself, to maintain your positive attributes and relationships with others while you rapidly advance your career. In a Harvard Business Review study, female CEOs scored significantly higher, in the 70th percentile, than the average for humility, the 55th.[xlix]

- **Let go of your ego.** Great CEOs have an "everyone wins" mentality, and their leadership style is about getting everyone to do their best. They must have a vision and strategic direction, but successful ones will stimulate the best also in their employees and teams around them as well.

- **Refuse to make excuses, and be willing to discuss failure.** Effective business leaders understand that making excuses is a waste of time and energy; it is more important to focus on next steps and a timeline for getting the job done. They are more likely to accept responsibility and look for ways to learn from the circumstances, because they are unafraid of failure. One way to become more comfortable with this is by actively learning from the past and adjusting plans and behaviors. A future CEO must have the ability to learn from past experiences and instill lessons for the future. You will learn that mistakes happen, and almost all can be fixed or accounted for.

- **Be personable.** CEOs should convey a personable demeanor, and one way to achieve this is by remaining humble and modest about their qualifications. A great leader is less self-involved, and more focused on developing future great leaders and CEOs.

A CEO I worked closely with for a number of years valued humility more than most traits. In fact, he led the charge, with his 300-person leadership team, on changing one of the four company values from "respect" to "humility," because he deemed it to be more important. His humility about his own performance stood out. For example, he always gave credit to those who mildly supported him on initiatives, when celebrating success, even when he was the driver of this success. I learned a lot about this personality trait from him. As his Chief of Staff, I was humbled every day by how little I knew about operating at an executive level. It taught me to let go of my ego, refuse to make excuses and be open to discussing failure, while being personable. It served as a reminder that I will continue to learn from and collaborate with those around me, even when I am at the executive level.

Drive, Curiosity, Humility, **Adaptability**.

Openness and Adaptability – *a combination of traits that balance each other out as you expand your horizons and accelerate your growth opportunities.*

- **Take risks.** CEOs who are successful in leading transformative change within a company (and sometimes within an entire industry) are able to embrace taking risks related to business decisions (like funding the development of a new product or ending a focus on a different part of the business) in a way that differs from the other Members of their leadership team.

  If you were raised in an environment that may have inhibited your appetite for risk, pay close attention to developing this trait. When I was growing up, my sister and I were encouraged to play it safe – to smile, sit like ladies and get all As. The boys I grew up with, on the other hand, were encouraged to play rough. My cousins scaled buildings, stayed out later at night and were allowed to whistle (in my family, whistling was not "ladylike"). They were encouraged to take risks and embrace ambiguity, while the girls curled themselves into risk aversion.

  If you have little girls or know someone who does, you have the opportunity to change the way women approach risk in the future, or rise to the top of any industry's pyramid. Tell them they are built to be a CEO.

But, as flight attendants say on airplanes, *put your air mask on before helping others.* A study published in the journal *Work, Employment and Society* in April 2018 showed that girls with working mothers get better jobs and higher pay. In fact, daughters of working mothers in the U.S. make about 23% more than daughters of stay-at-home mothers. And across the 25 developed countries represented in that survey, 21% of women whose mothers worked got supervisor jobs, compared to 18% of women who had stay-at-home mothers. Interestingly, the study showed that sons of working mothers grew up to spend eight more hours a week on household chores such as changing diapers and folding laundry – nearly double that of sons with stay-at-home moms.[1] Of course, the study did not imply that stay-at-home moms damage their children's futures, because there is no right way to raise a child. There is more value in focusing on the characteristics you build for yourself, which could then be reflected in your child. For example, you could approach risk in a different way to develop a trait like adaptability.

- **Be courageous.** Courage can be defined as taking risks in the face of fear. Taking calculated risks shows confidence and helps you grow as a business leader. Often, risky decisions may take you on a fresh, significant path to accelerate your career and help you overcome any fears of failing.
- **Embrace obstacles.** A true CEO understands that obstacles are a part of the path to more success. CEOs may even see obstacles as an opportunity to learn new skills or leverage a situation to their advantage. By embracing obstacles, you will build the emotional stamina to go against the grain – take risks, not just talk about them. In Harvard Business Review sample, CEOs who considered setbacks to be failures had a

50% smaller chance of thriving. Aspiring CEOs who demonstrated a positive attitude for adaptability and their mistakes were more likely to summit the corporate ladder.

- **Acclimate proactively.** Highly adaptable CEOs regularly plug into broader streams of information: they scan wider networks and diverse sources of data to actively anticipate challenges. As a result, these leaders will sense change earlier and deploy strategic steps to ensure their business is protected and could even thrive. Most CEOs know they have to divide their attention among short-, medium- and long-term perspectives, but the adaptable CEOs spent significantly more of their time – as much as 50% – thinking about the long term.

In summary, there are four key traits that will accelerate your growth opportunities on your path to becoming a CEO – drive, curiosity, humility and adaptability. These traits mostly work together; they certainly work better when they are all being developed in order to head in one direction, which is what I will cover in this next section.

2. Traits that align personal goals with professional goals.

Ask yourself, "To what extent do I possess this trait?"

Being Purposeful – *an introspective personality trait that applies intentional, focused and deeper meaning to actions.*

- **Find your purpose.** According to McKinsey, CEOs tend to show a greater sense of purpose and passion for what they do than other Members of company leadership. Ask your colleagues what they perceive as their professional purpose. Ask them if they know what yours is, or what it could be.

- **Defend and share your purpose.** Future CEOs should develop an ability to stand their ground and speak their minds, even if their opinion could be unpopular. The way you navigate difficult situations like these will determine how your purpose is communicated and perceived. Don't be afraid to sprinkle a bit of heart into your conversation – express vulnerability and affection even in conflict.
- **Connect with the culture.** One characteristic commonly overlooked is the importance of connecting with the culture and people that make up an organization. Do not be the leader who remains distant and removed from the people who are the DNA of the organization; try to actively and personally connect with and embody the organization's intended culture as a way to cultivate trust.

In my early career, when I was first applying for full-time jobs, I was fortunate enough to receive offers from consulting firms, banks and start-ups. From my previous internship experiences – especially that at the United Nations – I was able to define the meaningful impact I would like to have. For me, this was to continue to develop business acumen while giving back to the community I lived in, ideally by supporting gender equity, income equity and environmental protection. I then joined a not-for-profit organization called AAA Northern California, Nevada, Utah (AAA NCNU) – a part of the American Automobile Association. AAA NCNU invented the stop sign in the name of road safety and became the number-one provider of emergency road service across the United States. In 2018, it invested in launching the largest electric car sharing fleet in America at the time – citing the service advantages for its Members and community and the environmental benefits. It also acquired the largest autonomous vehicle testing site in America, to spearhead research and testing for creating safer roads. I have not even once regretted joining, because the organization prioritized making a positive impact on the vast community it serves, and enabled its employees to commit their time to this at work and outside. At organizations like AAA NCNU, it is easier to find and contribute to your purpose.

Purposeful, **Passionate**, Engaging.

Being Passionate – *an outward-looking personality trait that aims to create more energy around a topic, goal or vision.*

- **Find your passion.** The best CEOs are passionate about their work. Passion derives from a strong connection to your mission, your vision and your goals. It is what you get when you mix your purpose with your drive and emotions. Without that passion and connection, it can be challenging to understand a company's nitty-gritty, potentially boring operational details, and why it operates in the way it does. Passion will also naturally maintain your focus on getting things done.
- **Be kind.** When you find your passion and drive toward it, it can be easy to forget that not everyone shares your passion, and not everyone exists to help you pursue what you are aiming for. I value and respect kindness greatly outside work, as well as at every level in an organization. Note that being driven and being kind are not mutually exclusive. In a company I spent years at, one of its leadership principles was "never let a peer fail," not only as a business objective, but also as an extension of kindness and

passion. Practice empathy and promote internal, cross-functional collaboration.

- **Genuinely try to genuinely understand.** A CEO must be understanding of issues in and out of the workplace, and that some things happen outside of her or anyone else's control. Without genuine understanding, you may be distracted by frustration and impatience, and this may impact your passion and drive for overcoming an obstacle.

Purposeful, Passionate, **Engagement.**

Being Engaging – *an outward-looking personality trait that aims to focus energy on making an impact.*

- **Stay focused on results.** Once CEOs set a clear course for the business, they require support from employees and other stakeholders. A Harvard Business Review study found that CEOs who engaged stakeholders with this results orientation were 75% more successful in the role. While life may be "about the journey, not the destination," in a business environment, the destination (and the incentives attached to it) can be inspiration for those who working toward it.
- **Invite others on the journey.** CEOs need the *continued* support of their employees and other stakeholders. Engage these stakeholders in planning and execution by highlighting their sense of purpose and ownership over the "why" and the "how." Craft disciplined communications and influencing strategies to guide you through this. Manage with purpose and passion, in the face of inevitable conflict; remember that you need the support of others, even though you are the top of the pyramid. In fact, when HBR analyzed leaders who employed an accelerated path to CEO, one of the

qualities that stood out was their willingness to engage in and solve conflict.

- **Coach someone.** The CEO is responsible for establishing company culture, the principles of succession planning and a collaborative work environment. CEOs prepare their Board of Directors and the world for the next generation – or future direction – of the company, as well as the next generation of CEO talent. As a future CEO, it will be helpful to start identifying the tools that make you and others around you successful. If you have the chance to be someone's coach, treasure this opportunity as a way to develop a future CEO in yourself and others. The best managers are also the best listeners – offer mentorship and guidance whenever possible.

In summary, the traits that you develop to accelerate your growth opportunities will work more seamlessly when your professional and personal goals are aligned. The last set of traits that you should begin cultivating early are those that make CEOs successful in their roles.

3. Traits that successful CEOs exhibit

In Chapter 1 of this book, and based on my experience working very closely with multiple CEOs, I summarize the function of a CEO into these four key points:

- **The CEO owns the vision** – She determines and communicates the organization's strategic direction, which all other decisions are based on. Without this, the company is merely a collection of humans pursuing individual goals, guided by their own values.
- **The CEO balances resources** – She controls three of the corporate world's most important resources –

capital, people and her time – to drive the company's success.

- **The CEO strengthens the culture** – She establishes and shares the set of shared attitudes, goals, behaviors and values that characterize the people that represent the company.
- **The CEO makes the decisions** – While some final decisions may be up to the CEO's boss (the Board of Directors), she uses the vision, sources and culture she has established to execute strategy and deliver performance.

Based on a number of interactions and personal experiences observing CEOs from my Chief of Staff role, there are a few key traits that help CEOs perform effectively in the role, and be considered successful.

Bigger Picture Creativity
- **Create a "vision" for every project.** Without vision, a CEO is merely a celebrated facilitator or a seasoned manager. Since the CEO owns the vision for a company, you can start by owning the vision for what you are accountable for – your current projects. For each of your projects, continue exploring and nurturing the vision and ways of testing the vision in the real world by soliciting feedback from others and learning from your mistakes. Work on being able to compellingly communicate that vision to inspire, motivate and lead others to contribute to its success. To improve or develop a vision, surround yourself with others who have big visions. [li]
- **Think strategically and outside the box.** A great CEO can take ownership of the strategic direction of a company and should be able to model the vision for the company with actions, not just words. On your path to

CEO, you will learn quickly that tried-and-true methods do not always work. Continue to research personal improvement skills, learn from other executives or invest in a business mentor. Employ more unconventional training methods for thinking outside the box, like committing yourself to always voicing the craziest idea you can think of in situations like group discussions or brainstorms. The most transformative ideas are those that initially sound difficult or impossible to accomplish and potentially unbelievable. Imagine how much a room of people from the 1980s would have laughed at the idea of making a phone that would fit in someone's pocket?

- **Stay somewhat organized.** Being creative does not mean being a scatterbrain. Some CEOs might not be organized in the conventional sense – they may not have a tidy desk or desktop. However, successful CEOs take logical steps to solving problems within the business. The next time you encounter a challenge or obstacle, organize your thinking to determine the root cause, a list of priority actions and a definition of noise or distractions that could obstruct you from solving the core issue.

I worked closely with a CEO who knew, unmistakably, the bigger picture that he desired for the company – so much so that he was able to name a few employees among the thousands he had met that had the traits needed for what he desired. And despite his ability to be a visionary and a thinker, he also cultivated the ability to stay exceptionally organized with his black binder, where he amassed his to-do list. (He once admitted this black binder was older than I was. He then asked me if I could teach him how to digitally create to-do lists on his work computer. He was always looking for opportunities to improve.)

Another executive I worked closely with, and someone I consider a mentor in the workplace, was also able to lucidly identify visionary and out-of-the-box-thinking traits. She once told me she did not organically have the traits described, so she repeatedly hired people that showed a natural ability to operate with them.

Grit.
This is what it means to manage different stakeholders and resources, and use logic and reasoning to justify even controversial actions.

- **Be bold.** Effective CEOs are visionary, strong communicators and culture builders. They make fact-based judgments but also form strong points of view on issues that matter. Practice voicing your opinions; you may want to engage in open dialogues, gather diverse points of view and listen to other opinions to get more comfortable with doing this. The more practice you have with making tough decisions for a project or people, the more equipped you will be as a future CEO.
- **Develop finely-tuned intuition:** Great CEOs follow their intuition and commit to their beliefs. Their inner voice steers the company in the direction they dictate. This will come more naturally with experience, but you can start now by documenting situations that have taught you leadership lessons.
- **Be unafraid of the trenches.** Effective CEOs refuse to hide away in their corner office. They take every opportunity to observe or engage with their teams in action. They treasure first-hand knowledge because it links them more closely to the client, customer or Member their company serves.

A (former) CEO I worked closely with for over a year taught me a lesson on grit when he merged his company with a far larger organization. He made this bold move because he believed it was the right thing to do. He also knew in advance that in situations where companies merge, one CEO usually exits – and that would likely be him. Instead of shying away from the merger, he persisted with negotiations *and* sought to prove to the future leaders of the new company that his unique intuition was needed, and that he was not afraid of the trenches (in what could be his new role in the future state of the company). He became the new CEO's trusted advisor for years.

Decisiveness

- **Don't be scared.** Top performing CEOs are not afraid of, and may even enjoy, making critical decisions on a daily basis, and bearing the risk of making bad decisions. To become more comfortable with this, try to size up a situation, analyze the pros and cons and then make a decision that can be reversed, adjusted or mitigated. Among CEOs who were fired over issues related to decision-making, only 35% lost their jobs because they made "bad calls" – the majority were terminated for being indecisive. [lii]
- **Decide with speed and conviction**: Harvard Business Review uncovered that high-performing CEOs are not necessarily respected for making the correct decisions; rather, they are set apart for being more decisive. They make decisions earlier, quicker and persuade others of its validity in the face of ambiguity. Studies show that people who were described as "decisive" were 12 times more likely to be high-performing CEOs. [liii]
- **Don't wait for perfect information.** Smart but slow decision-makers sometimes create bottlenecks within a company, and are a source of frustration for teams who are able to move faster. Studies show that out of the executives who were rated poor on decisiveness,

85

only 6% received low marks because they made decisions *too quickly*. The rest scored badly because they took too long to make decisions. [liv]

When I was Chief of Staff, I once gifted the CEO a giant, red button that screamed "NO!" in different voices for Christmas. (One of the voice options even sounded like mine.) It was a reminder to not wait for perfect information in order to make a decision, especially if that decision is "no." At the time, the CEO was trying to push away projects that distracted the company from its vision. I encouraged him to keep the button accessible so he would be reminded to dismiss distracting projects early, with speed and conviction, without waiting for "perfect" information. I thought it might help make quicker decisions.

Emotional intelligence
- **Be trustworthy.** Trust is key to collaboration and building strong networks. Start by forging mutually beneficial relationships. CEOs are not necessarily extroverted but can effectively decipher emotions and are usually approachable, warm and reliable. In *Chapter 7: The Agenda Drivers*, I discuss how to build trust among those around you in detail.
- **Communicate effectively.** Great CEOs will communicate in a simple and clear form, avoiding company jargon and egotistical content. Their messages inspire and motivate while conveying information in language that keeps parties neutral, does not instigate conflict and is easily understandable. In order to do this, they must listen to determine what their audience cares about. To develop this skill as a future CEO, start by structuring your communication in a B.L.U.F – Bottom Line Up Front, followed by three key attributes of your

message and ending on an inspiring note that rests on what your audience is looking for. I learned this recommended communication structure from more than one CEO I worked closely with.

- **Hire the right people**. The success of a CEO is hardly ever attributed to just her achievements – there is often a team that made her vision a reality. Effective CEOs will surround themselves with strong teams to free themselves to focus on vision, culture and big picture decision-making. A hiring manager is often inclined to hire someone based on her immediate needs as opposed to a candidate's future potential. The golden rule for hiring people is to look for someone who could be your boss one day. Take notes on the lesson I learned from a stellar human resources executive, Sue Hagen – "6s hire 4s, and 8s hire 10s···and 6s don't know they're 6s." So, if you hire someone who is more likely to merely get the job done, versus someone who could be your future boss, you are a 6 out of 10 as a leader. You can change this by hiring people who will grow to be better than you are.

Being trustworthy, communicating effectively and hiring the right people are traits and skills that may not come naturally to everyone. It requires years of practice. A CEO I worked for taught me lessons in emotional intelligence when I witnessed him, time and time again, give ownership of important decisions to others who possessed far less knowledge than him on a subject. I imagine this was painful for him – he was usually right and certainly valued making a correct decision. But his intuition, and superior emotional intelligence, led him to allow others to feel ownership over decisions. These situations often worked out the way he intended, and the risks he took and trust he built made him a better business leader.

In order to be an effective CEO, you also have to look beyond personality types, and into what personality traits will accelerate your career, align your personal and professional goals and help you become a successful CEO. Personality types are a roundabout way of looking at what you have and do not have. They show what you over-index in. Focusing on developing *traits* will save you time and effort; as you do this, you will know right away what your limiting factors are. Then you can begin to work on developing and exemplifying these traits, on your journey to becoming a CEO.

Chapter 5
A List of Excuses

You can have results or excuses. Not both.

Before you are ready to dive into building your resume, pushing your agenda and crafting your path forward, you must acknowledge that you will need to work through multiple challenges that impede your journey to CEO. One that you can overcome today are excuses. These blockers are in your control. This chapter will prepare you for how to overcome any excuse that may slow you down.

Picture this···

Everyone has met, worked for or worked with someone who doesn't deliver – someone who typically defaults to one of the following excuses.

1. You didn't tell me you needed that
2. I didn't understand
3. I don't know how
4. I didn't think it was important
5. There was an emergency
6. You should have asked someone else
7. You're being too hard on me
8. I forgot
9. You never do what I ask you to do, either
10. Nobody else is doing that
11. Someone told me I didn't need to do it
12. That's not my job
13. You could have done it yourself
14. I did do it, but I guess you didn't get my note/email
15. I didn't have time

Terrible, right? Excuses destroy relationships and evaporate credibility. A CEO I worked for always reminded me that the currency of the workplace is not money or years of experience. The currency of the business world that functions as a meritocracy is *credibility*, because you deal credibility in exchange for information, goods, services and promotions.

I learned the transactional nature of credibility in the workplace while I was Chief of Staff. I made almost every mistake in that role over two years. I was lucky though – I started at around a 75% score of credibility, where the CEO trusted me with most tasks; in many other companies, you start with an under 50% score and the expectation is that you prove yourself and earn credibility points. In fact, when I made a mistake in the role, I could virtually *feel* credibility points being taken away from me. It was like someone walked up to me, stuck their large palm out just below eye-level and gestured that I reach into my pocket and hand over what was rightfully theirs. One time, my team and I sent the CEO the wrong version of a document for him to review before a five-hour plane ride. He downloaded the document at the airport and planned to evaluate it while he was in the air. We not able to reach him on the plane to alert him that we were going to send a replacement; there was no excuse that would give him back his time.

Oftentimes, we are embarrassed for and frustrated by people who lack credibility and make excuses. This leads me to my next point – here are a list of common excuses for shying away from the CEO position. The following list is organized by the nature of the scapegoat:

(1) Personality and Background
(2) Universal
(3) Circumstantial

Personality and Background Excuses

- **I am not the Meyers Briggs CEO personality type.** See *Chapter 4* that emphasizes traits over types.
- **I come from a poor background.** Some of the most successful people started with very little in their pockets. For example, Oprah Winfrey was born into a poor family in Mississippi, but this did not stop her from winning a scholarship to Tennessee State University and becoming the first African American TV correspondent in the state at the age of 19. In 1983, Oprah moved to Chicago to work for what became *The Oprah Winfrey Show*, and boasts a net worth of $2.7 billion. Money can often make it easier to achieve your goals, but the key ingredient is resourcefulness. In fact, when I interned at the Harvard Admissions Office during my days as an undergrad, I heard the Dean of Admissions at the time repeatedly say, "75% of our students are on some form of financial aid. When we find stellar candidates who exemplify resourcefulness, we'll make sure they can attend."
- **I'm not educated enough.** I am a firm believer that nobody is educated enough, and that education is not necessarily something you learn at school. In fact, experiential learning can be far more valuable and engaging, and this has been evident for over a century. Pioneering cosmetics entrepreneur Helena Rubinstein built her $60 million business in the early 20th century without a college degree, after doing bookkeeping for her father, a wholesale food broker. She showed an appetite for understanding numbers and, at age 15, attended her first business meeting in place of her ill father.
- **I didn't have the right teachers.** There are only a few skills on this planet that you cannot teach yourself,

especially in the age of the internet – a free and unlimited resource at your fingertips. In fact, if you find yourself talking about the "right" teacher or mentor, you are already placing an excessive amount of value and emphasis on others versus yourself. You are your best teacher; set time to teach yourself, reflect and improve. The next few chapters will dig into how to find mentors and discover the mentor in yourself. In *Chapter 9: The Support Boosters,* I will feature some of my most influential mentors, and what to look for in a role model.

- **I'm not destined to succeed.** Everything that ultimately happens in your life is due, in part, to the decisions you make. Refer to *Chapter 10: Your Path(s) Forward* for some tried-and-true paths for career success.

- **I'm not ready.** You can never be prepared to get started. If it means learning more will prevent you from failure, then you are wrong. You will make mistakes and simply learning more will fool you into thinking you are making progress when in fact it is simply a buffer from taking action.

- **I'm not motivated enough.** If you lack the drive to do whatever it is you hope to do, there is a chance that you do not yearn for your goals enough or view it as a goal. In *Chapter 1: Do You Want To Be CEO?* and *Chapter 2: Time is your MVP*, I will dive into the types of goals and how to set them high enough.

- **I can't handle failure.** We are rejected every day of our lives, but we fail to see the rejections because we do not choose to acknowledge them. Learn to detach yourself from outcomes and to see the process as journey of self-discovery. Refer to *Chapter 7: The Agenda Drivers.* While I was writing version three of this book, which took me approximately two weeks to work through, my hard drive was wiped in some kind of freak accident and I lost what I had been working on. I will admit – I considered giving up many times that day. I am glad I did not. I do not regret picking up from scratch.

- **I'm too easily distracted by other things.** There are always going to be things around us that are more fun and exciting. But the key here is to be disciplined and to dedicate a certain period of your time to advance your goals. To understand the cost behind distractors, refer to *Chapter 2: Time is your MVP.*

- **I am scared.** There will always be fear. The most successful people in the world are fearful of something, but they have the courage to move past the fear. Fear is a good thing. Fear means it is a big enough goal that is worth pursuing. If you set a goal that does not scare you then you might as well take it off the list, because it will be easy to abandon. From there, turn your fear into excitement. Tell yourself, "Challenge accepted."

- **It's just who I am.** This is a self-fulfilling prophecy. If you believe it, then it is true. If you think you are not tall enough to be successful, then you will not be. If you think you are not built to reach your goals, then you will not. If not reaching your goals is who you are, try changing your belief to "reaching my goals is who I am." It's just like Henry Ford said, "Whether you think you can, or think you can't, you're right." You are built to change your story, change your actions and change your life.

- **It's too hard.** I tell my colleagues in the turbulent startup world all the time: "It's not supposed to be easy." If achieving your goals was that easy then everyone would be doing it. Everything you want in life takes work. It involves doing things we do not want to do. If it is hard then it is a good sign that you will not get bored. I could not tell you how many goals I pushed off my plate because they were too easy. A hard goal is stimulating and engaging.

- **I've already dedicated myself to a different path.** It is never too late to change paths. Just because you are on one road does not mean you cannot take a different path and pursue a different journey.
- **I'm just not lucky enough.** All of us are lucky all of the time. The difference is that you just do not see the opportunities presented to you. To see opportunities presented to you, your mindset about luck needs to change.

Universal Excuses

- **I don't have the time.** All the most successful people in the world – CEOs, presidents and you – have the same 24 hours in a day. Examine closely how you spend your time and you will see where your priorities truly lie. There are very few commitments in this life that are truly non-negotiable. Refer to *Chapter 2: Time is your MVP.*

  Recall Bollywood actress Priyanka Chopra's speech when she was honored at Variety's Power of Women for her work with UNICEF. She described a time where her most trusted companions gifted her the "I don't have the time" excuse, but she refused it. She said:

  > A few years ago, I was shooting for Don 2. It was chosen to be shown at Berlin Film Festival. But at the same time, I was invited for the first time to attend the Grammy Awards in LA. It was a big choice. Both the events were literally taking place one day apart in completely different time zones. Everyone told me that I will have to choose. But you know what I did? I made

some insane connections and flew from Mumbai to London, London to Berlin, Berlin to Amsterdam, Amsterdam to LA and back to Mumbai in three days. I made it happen. Because I don't want anyone to tell me that I can't have everything.

Her speech inspired many around the world on social media to apply her time management to their own situations.

An example closer to me involves Jennifer Botterill, a mentor of mine, who must have more than 24 hours in her day. Jennifer is a master of time management. She is graduate of Harvard University and completed her degree with honors while she won four medals at the Olympics. She also played hockey for Harvard and is the only two-time winner of the Patty Kazmaier award (given to the top player in women's college hockey). She still holds the NCAA records for most consecutive games with a point and for most points in a hockey career. In addition to her hockey career and mentorship programs, she is also a keynote speaker, works in television with CBC and TSN and is a mother of two. She makes time for what she is built to be.

- **I've never done this before.** You have succeeded at loads of things that you had never done before. Every journey starts with the first step, but you have to take it. You never walked before you did, never drove a car before you first got behind the wheel and never had a job before you got your first one.
- **I don't have the skills.** I have one word of advice for people who live by this excuse: *Google*. On the internet, you can find instructions, how-tos and even books and courses on how to do practically anything for free. If you still cannot find what you need,

consider asking an expert online or purchasing a book on the topic.

- **I am overwhelmed.** The grand scheme of a goal can be daunting. No matter the size of the goal, the goal itself may appear so large that you do not know how to get started. It'll be easier to focus on the minor tasks that will get you to your goal. Focus on the process. For example, let us say your goal is to lose 30 lbs in 30 days. Focus on losing one pound per day rather than the overall goal. If you concentrate on the daily goals, you will incrementally move toward the mission you set out for. Refer to *Chapter 2: Time is your MVP.*

- **What if I fail?** What if you succeed? Failure is always a risk. Very few things have a 100% success rate. These defenses are all in your head, and part of a story you are telling yourself. Once you acknowledge these stories, you can begin to write your new story and get closer to your goals. Once you reach that goal, it will feel that much better knowing you overcame your defenses.

- **I was told I could not do it.** Very few amazing, innovative, revolutionary ideas have been borne out of group consensus. You will always encounter people who do not believe in you. Make an active effort to remind yourself that their opinions do not matter. If you allow the opinions of others to shape your confidence and your outlook, you may be waving goodbye to your dreams. In high school, my chemistry teacher told my parents that I should not continue to study chemistry after I failed a *midterm* exam. I am glad I did not drop the class, because I got an A in the end.

- **I haven't created anything new.** Some of the most successful businesses did not invent something completely new. Take something that already exists and improve on it, change it, tweak it, turn it around and give it your own spin.

- **It's too risky.** There is risk involved in everything. Understand your appetite for risk first. Are you someone who prefers a 1% return on U.S. Treasuries instead of the 7% to 10% you will probably get in the stock market? What would it take for you to try a different investment strategy?

  When I think something is too risky, I remember a story Patti Lee told me. It usually diminishes my "risky" problem. Patti was one of just a few reporters on scene when the Boston Marathon bomber was taken into custody in 2013. She reported live for hours during the manhunt and even dodged bullets directed at the bomber in Watertown, MA. Patti has literally fought off attacks in the field without missing her deadline.

- **If it were easy, everyone would do it.** Nothing is easy without the right support systems and mindset. Although everyone is built for success, only a few reach their goals. A big part of achievement is identifying what you need to succeed, and then going after it.

- **I don't have the support.** While having the support is beneficial, it will not be the reason for your success and is simply enough for getting you through hard times. The biggest things that matter in your journey toward success and achievement is your drive and motivation.

Circumstantial Excuses

- **I will start tomorrow.** If you genuinely have the time to do something now, you should. Use this opportunity to go and do it. You will feel a lot more energized and motivated knowing you have pushed yourself and made progress. The number one reason for employee happiness is getting something done.

- **I don't have the money.** You will not have *enough* money even when you are CEO. Successful people understand that money is a resource that can grow, with the right strategies in place. For example, could you invest your money as a nest egg for a future endeavor, or could you take out a loan or apply for a grant? The really successful people will remember that time is a more valuable resource than money, whether it is invested or not, and time is money.
- **The conditions aren't right.** Things may never be *perfect*. Many things were launched at the wrong time or before the world was ready. Some of them failed, and some succeeded beyond anybody's wildest dreams. Waiting for the right conditions is like the fisherman sitting on the banks, waiting for the fish, but never putting his hook in the water.
- **It's not the right time.** There is never a right time to start. The only time to start is right now. Do it while you are still breathing, because something will always come up: an unexpected bill, chore or child. Only a few things in life hurt more than regret.
- **I don't have enough time to discover what I like.** If you sit down and make a list of all the things you do in a typical day, you will begin to realize that you may have enough time. Determine what is wasting your time and replace it with the things that will get you to your goals.

Benjamin Franklin said, "Tell me and I forget. Teach me and I may remember, involve me and I learn." It is time for you to pick the excuses above that made you feel awkward – the ones you have heard and may have even used.[lv]

This chapter may have caused anxiety and some fear. That is normal. You may encounter much more anxiety and fear on your path to CEO. Just know that being or feeling defeated is temporary; giving up is permanent.

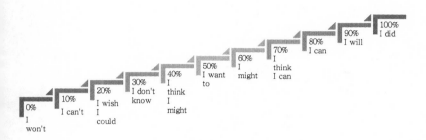

100%
I did

90%
I will

80%
I can

70%
I think
I can

60%
I might

50%
I want
to

40%
I think
I might

30%
I don't
know

20%
I wish
I could

10%
I can't

0%
I won't

SECTION 2
Your Game Plan

In the next four chapters, I will dive deep into a few key lessons that are not often taught in college or graduate school, but could be instrumental in shaping your path to becoming a CEO.

Chapter 7: The Resume Builders

Chapter 8: The Agenda Drivers

Chapter 9: The Support Boosters

Chapter 10: The Cherry on Top

The final chapter of this book will outline the paths you could utilize and navigate to get to the top.

Chapter 6
Your Game Plan:
The Resume Builders

This chapter rewinds to an essential resume builder – one that you must have before becoming a CEO, and one that I recommend you build in your early career: corporate finance knowledge.

Without corporate finance knowledge, your resume is unlikely to be considered for senior management roles. This is because most senior roles require you to manage a relatively large percentage of the company's money, and the leaders that would elect you to this role – likely the CEO or the Board of Directors – have a vested interest in ensuring the company makes responsible financial decisions.

And there is strong evidence to suggest that an early foundation in the finance industry is a factor in creating future CEOs. The CEO selection process, usually managed by the Board of Directors, favors extensive experience in finance-focused roles. Approximately 30% of Fortune 500 CEOs spent the first few years of their careers developing a strong foundation in finance, while 20% of CEOs began in sales and marketing roles.[lvi]

Unfortunately, females have been historically underrepresented in the finance industry. Oliver Wyman surveyed 850 financial services professionals and interviewed 100 senior female executives. The results pointed to a culture of sexism in the finance industry in the 1980s and 1990s that deterred women from joining the profession. Even millennial women who were surveyed admitted that the shift from university to the finance industry was a culture shock. The Wyman study also revealed that this culture has changed surprisingly little in the U.S. over the past decades. The sad truth is that unconscious biases and gender role expectations create career disadvantages for women still linger in different industries. The majority of my female classmates from Harvard college started their careers in the finance industry, and have recalled stories of sexism and elitism. I won't share these here because they are extremely personal, but I recommend asking the women around you in the finance industry if they have had similar experiences.

In preparation for your journey to CEO, this chapter is a summary of how to count, track and spend money effectively in public, private and not-for-profit companies. Albert Einstein said, "Everything should be made as simple as possible, but not simpler." In the spirit of this, I have simplified almost everything you need to know about corporate finance into a seven-part case study about the rise and fall of UniMoose.

Part 1: UniMoose is founded

The CEO has founded a new company called UniMoose. The company rescues, trains and grooms moose that are not acclimating to the changing environment, as other mystical species emerge in the forest.

The CEO goes through the paperwork and processes of obtaining its licenses and permits, and is faced with two key accounting decisions. These accounting decisions will determine how the company will count and track the money it makes.

What type of accounting will it use? Based on the company's location and business type, it will choose between:

1. *Financial (statement) Accounting,* using the complex number-counting rules outlined in one of the two options:

   a. U.S. GAAP – written by the FASB (Financial Accounting Standards Board)

   b. IFRS (International Financial Reporting Standards) – written by the IASB (International Accounting Standards Board)

2. *Tax Accounting,* which focuses on taxes rather than the appearance of public financial statements.

3. *Management Accounting,* which uses financial *and* non-financial information (such as risk and opportunity for shareholders) to account for money.

What method will the company use to count money?

- *The Cash Method* – Revenues are recognized when collected, and expenses are recognized when paid. It is a simple method, but financial statements will be impacted by anomalies like late payments.

- *The Accrual Method (preferred)* – Revenues are recognized when earned, and expenses are matched to revenues (or the time period they relate to). This is a more accurate representation of a time period where money is made and spent because it removes anomalies.

Our CEO chose to report UniMoose's finances through financial accounting (U.S. GAAP) because that is what other companies in the industry use. The company will also use the accrual method to count money, as it wants financial statements to reflect the revenue expected and earned in the month. It chose to not use the cash method because it expects some clients and vendors will be late on payments.

UniMoose then hires external accountants to set up accounting processes and to provide an unbiased view of how they think the CEO should count money going forward. The company also hires internal auditors who act as in-house watchdogs and set up "internal controls," or rules for counting money, going forward.

Now UniMoose needs to decide how to track and spend its money.

Part 2: UniMoose begins its financial planning process

The company decides that it will follow a simple sequence for budgeting that most companies use. Budgeting is the process of creating a plan to spend money. Producing this spending plan allows the CEO to determine in advance whether she will have enough money to do the things she would like to do to make UniMoose successful.

Before building her budget, she considers the following things with her finance team to evaluate her financial needs.

1. *The Sales Budget* – what do we need to spend to sustain gross sales and revenue? The sales budget contains an itemization of a company's sales expectations for the budget period. It is extremely important to do the best possible job of forecasting both in units sold and in dollars, since the information in the sales budget is used by the other budgets.

2. *The Production and Expense Budget* – what do we need to spend on to drive sales? For example, a marketing department will need to spend on advertisements, packaging and new product development.

3. *The Capital Budget* – what additional money do we need to grow the company? A business determines and evaluates potential large expenses or investments. These include projects such as building a new facility or investing in a long-term venture.

4. *The Financing Budget* – how are we going to ensure our money is working to make more money? For example, how much should we invest in the stock market, or in other venture capital funds, to earn income on the side?

5. *The Cash Flow Projection* – how can we validate that we have made the right decisions for our budget? For example, are there other ways of predicting the flow of cash in and out to end up at the same final number?

6. *The Pro Forma Balance Sheet* – how can we maintain a standardized and fact-based process for allocating money? Businesses use pro forma statements for decision-making in planning and control, and for external reporting to owners, investors and creditors.

The CEO of UniMoose maps out its financial needs for funding sales, production, capital and financing. She is then informed by her accountants that she has another budget decision to make – what budgeting *methodology* will UniMoose go with?

She is presented with this table:

Type of Budget	Description
Responsibility Budgeting	Costs are charged or allocated to departments that make a profit for the company, to determine if they are really profitable.
Activity-based Budgeting	Links the budget to the activities performed by a department. For example, the human resources team budgets for training all new team members. This method helps determine the most effective use of the financial resources available.
Zero-based Budgeting	Builds the budget from a base of zero – which essentially means the company assumes it has no money. It requires that all expenses be justified and prioritized, and is therefore very time-consuming.
Flexible Budgeting	Adjusts variable costs in relationship to sales, which helps differentiate between "real" variances and volume-related variances.
Rolling Budget	As a quarter in the year is completed, the company adds a new quarter to the budget period.

UniMoose decides to keep things simple and stick with a rolling budget. This is because the business is small and new and does not need to plan beyond the year. It also sees the benefit of changing its budget allocations every quarter as it learns how to better operate the business over time.

Part 3: UniMoose begins to sell things

The company, now clear on how it will count and budget money, uses its accounting and budgeting methods to allocate money for selling its service – the training of North American moose (no animals were harmed in the making of this chapter).

UniMoose begins to track its financial performance using four financial statements (income statements, balance sheets, the retained earnings statement and the cashflow statement). To simplify operations, the company focuses mainly on two of the four – its **Income Statement (P&L)**, which measures performance over a period of time, and its **Balance Sheet,** which measures performance at a point in time.

1. Income Statement: (Revenues – Expenses = Profit or Loss)

UniMoose's income statement tells the organization whether it has made or lost money for a period of time. As the company expands, it could use this statement for inter-division performance measures, for valuing acquisitions and as a measure of its ability to pay debt.

Other companies may have other names for the income statement – the earnings statement, the P&L (profit and loss) statement or the operations statement. Sometimes, the terms income, profit, and earnings may be used interchangeably. For example, net income is the same as net profit or net earnings.

This is one of the most important documents the CEO of UniMoose looks at every month, as it confirms how the company performed in relation to what it planned for in the past, and frames what financial, operational or people changes need to occur to continue to perform well in the future.

Here is the form template that her company uses:

Income Statement Format		
	Gross sales or revenues	100
	– Returns, discounts and allowances	*–10*
	= Net sales or revenues	**90**
	– Cost of goods sold (cost of sales)	*–50*
	= Gross profit	**40**
	– Selling, general & administrative expenses	*–5*
	– Depreciation expense	*–5*
	– Research and development expense	*–5*
	= Operating profit	**25**
	+ Interest or investment income	5
	– Interest expense	*–2.5*
	+ / – Gain or loss from sale of assets	–2.5
	= Pre-tax income	**25**
	– Income tax	*–5*
	= Net Income	**20**

She compares these results to what she planned, as well as to previous month and previous year performance to judge whether her business performed well or not, and to what extent.

She also looks at other components that can help her make judgments on what she should do next to manage the business effectively:

- The EBIT (earnings before interest and tax) and EBITDA (earnings before interest, tax, depreciation and amortization). This measure is similar to other profitability ratios, but it can be especially useful for comparing companies with different capital investment, debt and tax profiles.

- The company's "margins," again, as gauges to compare itself to its competitors. For example:

  o **Gross margin** is gross profit divided by net sales. The higher the better, because it shows the costs of your goods or service are at a minimum, and you get to retain more of the money you made.

  o **Operating margin** is operating profit divided by net sales. Again, the higher the better, because it shows your administrative and other expenses are at a minimum, and you get to retain more of the money you made.

  o **Profit margin** is either pre-tax or net income divided by net sales. Again, the higher the better, because it shows the taxes you pay are at a minimum, and you get to retain more of the money you made.

These three key margins provide an indication about how your expenses are inhibiting your company's ability to keep the money it made. If UniMoose finds a competitor that has a much higher margin, then this competitor must have some kind of secret sauce for keeping its expenses low. Perhaps it keeps its cost of goods low because they are produced in bulk, or their administrative expenses low because they use automated machines over humans.

Currently, only one other company in the U.S. trains and rears North American moose. The CEO of UniMoose takes a class on how to evaluate the P&L/Income Statement. She learns that she should look at a few key things:

1. **How's revenue doing?** The "top line" of the P&L will tell her if the company's product is right for the consumer it is targeting.

2. **How do profits look?** She remembers her CFO's phrase, "revenues are vanity, profits are sanity," because impressive sales numbers are only meaningful if they can be turned into profits. This is at the bottom of the P&L. The net profit line tells us how much money the business has made after deducting all costs (that's why it's called "the bottom line"). It is also important to look a little further up the P&L at the operating profit line, which is arrived at by subtracting from revenues only the direct costs of making those sales (raw materials, wages and administrative costs).

3. **How are all of these factors performing** versus what was planned before the beginning of the year, what is being forecasted during the year and how the business performed the previous year, for the current month, the current quarter and the year to date.

As she continues to dig into the numbers, she schedules meetings with the accountable owners for different parts of the P&L, to determine what they can tweak and improve to drive the bottom line. She wants to grow the top line, keep expenses constant or low, and pay the minimum allowed amount of taxes, which will grow the bottom line. Ideally, some of that profit is available for reinvestment in the company or pay out higher bonuses to its employees.

2. Balance Sheet: (Assets = Liabilities + Equity)

The balance sheet shows UniMoose's financial position at a given point in time. It may also be called the statement of financial position. The balance sheet spells out what is called "the accounting equation," and is represented visually in the table below.

ASSETS (what the company owns) = LIABILITIES (debts)
+ EQUITY (the owners' share)
or
ASSETS − LIABILITIES = EQUITY (net worth)

Total Assets	Total Liabilities and Equity
Cash and cash equivalents	Accounts payable
Marketable securities	Accrued liabilities
Accounts receivable	Short-term debt
Inventory	Current maturity of long-term
Prepaid expenses	debt
Current Assets	**Current Liabilities**
Buildings	Long-term debt
Equipment	Other liabilities due after one year
(Less accumulated depreciation)	
Land	**Total Liabilities**
Net Fixed Assets	Common stock
	(Treasury stock)
Investments	Retained earnings
Intangible assets	Cumulative comprehensive income
Other Assets	**Total Stockholders' Equity**

The CEO of UniMoose, through her balance sheet, has a clear understanding of how much money the company has in different forms.

3. The Statement of Retained Earnings

This is a financial statement that outlines the changes in retained earnings for a specified period. Retained earnings is the accumulated net income of a company – the money the company gets to keep after expenses.

UniMoose has not been functioning for long, so its reporting of this is shallow and it will use the income statement over this statement to make business decisions.

The statement of retained earnings is also a statement it might show shareholders in the future (UniMoose does not have any yet) to show what happened to the retained earnings of the business during the year.

UniMoose's competitor, MooseTown, is a publicly traded company (it has shareholders) and does produce this financial statement in the form of a statement of "shareholders' equity." This statement shows the changes in all of the equity accounts on the balance sheet instead of just the retained earnings account.

4. The Statement of Cash Flow

This statement breaks UniMoose's cash flow down into three components: (1) Cash flow from or used in **operations**, (2) Cash flow from or used in **investments**, (3) Cash flow from or used in **financing**. The three components refer to the three ways UniMoose can make money. For example, operations could be the UniMoose marketing team running television ads about the importance of training moose to adapt to their environment; investments would be the money invested in investment firms like Goldman Sachs and the stock market to make income on the side for the company; financing (not used by UniMoose yet) would be the money borrowed from investors or banks in order to fund projects or run the company.

The CEO of UniMoose hears the term "free cash flow" when her finance team talks about this statement, which excites her. "Free cash?!" she says. Her finance team shake their heads. Her Chief Financial Officer (CFO) explains that "free cash flow" are the funds that are left after the firm has reinvested in its operations, like paying for additional moose trainers to host classes for moose on adapting their behavior to their changing environment and supporting new species like unicorns. Additionally, "free" means they are available for other expenses, like dividends, acquisitions, debt reduction, or share buybacks. "Free"is not what she thought it was, but she's satisfied to have learned something new.

"Free cash flow" can be calculated by taking the operating cash flow and subtracting the capital expenditures made in the year, which is shown in the investments section of the statement.

Net income
Non-cash expenses such as depreciation and amortization
Net decrease (increase) in receivables, inventory and prepaid expenses
Net increase (decrease) in payables and accrued liabilities
                Cash flow from/for operations

(Purchase of fixed assets)
(Investments in other companies)
Sale of assets
                Cash flow from/for investments

Borrowing funds
(Paying back debt)
Funds from sale of company's stock
(Buying back stock – treasury stock)
(Payment of dividends)
                Cash flow from/for financing
                Net cash increase/decrease
                Cash at beginning of year
                Cash at end of year

UniMoose hits a milestone – it generates its financial statements and "closes the books" for the first time. This means the company's finance team combined revenues and expenses to determine a profit, and transferred this profit to retained earnings (a pool of cash/investments the company considers an asset).

Following this, the team reflects on a few high-level questions to determine if the company is operating in a sustainable way, so that it is not giving away its profits too soon:

- **Is operating cash flow significantly more than what is spent on depreciation?** Depreciation is the expensing (recording a cost on a financial statement) of fixed assets, because they lose value. For example, the equipment used to transport moose in and out of the training areas will experience wear and tear, and are not worth as much as when they were first bought. Fixed assets are tangible.

  Amortization, on the other hand, is the practice of spreading an intangible asset's cost over that asset's useful life. Intangible assets are not physical assets. For example, the cost of the 2,000 DVDs bought, with hours of training material for each moose to watch, are amortized because the moose will watch this training material over time (potentially a 6-month course). The higher the operating cash flow and the less spent on depreciation, the better.

- **Are funds being reinvested in the business?** Is the reinvestment greater than the depreciation expense for the year? This question essentially asks if you are putting money in places that will create value for the company, like in developing training programs, versus places where you lose money because of wear and tear, like in more materials for transporting moose. If UniMoose was spending more in depreciation than in research and development functions, it would signal that the business could stagnate in the future. The CEO, after encountering this signal, should feel encouraged to shift where her company is investing its retained earnings.

- **Is the firm paying dividends?** If so, what percentage of the profits are being paid out? Is that percentage realistic and sustainable? This question essentially gauges whether the company is giving too much (money that could be better spent reinvested in the company) back to its owners and shareholders. UniMoose does not have any shareholders and therefore does not pay dividends yet.

As UniMoose grows, it explores "tax-loss harvesting" or "tax-loss selling," to reduce the taxes it pays and operate in an even more sustainable way. This is an effort to keep more of the money it has made instead of giving it away through high tax payments. Learning about tax-loss harvesting can be one of those head-tilting moments because it requires you to go against your gut and sell certain investment assets at a loss, which will in turn reduce the taxes you owe at the end of the year. *A little complicated, I know*, but this strategy is a useful tool.

Meanwhile, at the end of the year, MooseTown publishes its annual report. As a publicly held firm, it included a letter to its shareholders, a review of operations, Management Discussion and Analysis (MD&A), historical data and public relations information. The report was read by the Board, management, shareholders, government, taxation authorities, prospective shareholders, lenders, prospective lenders, employees, vendors, customers and security analysts. UniMoose also read MooseTown's annual report in order to scope out its main competition in a market that it hopes to dominate.

Part 4: UniMoose plans to grow

In order to accelerate its growth, UniMoose needs more money. It hires a Board of Directors, consisting of a group of five experts from different backgrounds, to advise on strategy and provide oversight and insight to the CEO. Before it determines which short-term and long-term financing methods it will utilize, it considers these six factors:

1. **Type of organization** (public, private, not-for-profit) – it is private.
2. **The amount of money required for use now and later** – it needs $1 billion now, for projects it is ready to execute, and $2 billion later, for projects it plans to execute when the time is right. North American moose are expensive to rear and train.
3. **The time period the money is needed for, and how long is it supposed to last** – it decides that the first sum will be spread over 10 years.
4. **The planned use for the money** – it will invest in facilities for transporting these moose from nature preserves across the country, not just within the state. It also hopes to establish a set of rules for the humane treatment of these animals, and will need to hire teams to certify locations before UniMoose trades with them.
5. **The business's financial health** – UniMoose's finance team determines the business is healthy because it is making a comfortable profit and has no debt.
6. **The financial markets and economic environment** – moose rescues are considered trendy: there is high demand for this service, and UniMoose anticipates competition only from MooseTown.

As a result of this evaluation, UniMoose decides to explo both short-term and long-term financing options.

Short-term Financing helps the business with immediate operational needs, like hosting moose classes or buying food for the moose. Short-term financing is listed under the "current liabilities" section of the balance sheet. Here are some examples UniMoose explored:

1. *Trade credit* (accounts payable) – when one business pays the other's bills for a short period of time, until the business that owes money has access to funding. For example, the vendor that provides UniMoose with the special moose food it uses will continue to deliver food to the UniMoose facilities, because it knows the moose need the food and that UniMoose will pay them back for it soon.

2. *Short-term bank financing* – most organizations have an allowance to spend money they don't have, called a line of credit or revolving credit agreement, with their bank(s). UniMoose might take out a line of credit to pay for more seasoned trainers for the first month of the year, when the moose are finding it difficult to stick to their new year's resolutions.

3. *Commercial paper* – these are short term unsecured "notes," normally issued by large creditworthy public companies. The notes are similar to loans. They are also negotiable and may be bought and sold on the money market. Typically, a business will use commercial paper because the interest rate is lower than at the bank. UniMoose might use commercial paper from a public company that also trains unruly animals, if they were able to negotiate the interest rate down.

4. *Receivables-based financing* – this is a type of asset-financing arrangement where UniMoose could use its receivables (outstanding invoices or money owed by customers) to receive financing. UniMoose would

receive an amount that is equal to a reduced value of the receivables that were pledged. For example, if some clients have not paid for their training yet, UniMoose could get the amount that it is owed in financing, as the bank knows the moose and their supporters will pay UniMoose soon for their training services.

5. *Inventory-based financing* – This is used for companies with inventory. If UniMoose had inventory, like self-help books and moose-nuzzles, it would borrow money to pay for the inventory, often from a finance company owned by the manufacturer. When the inventory is sold, the loan is repaid.

The CEO of UniMoose is holding off on making a decision until it evaluates its long-term financing options – it believes its planned use for the additional $1 billion in funds is a long-term strategic play.

Long-term Financing is typically used to pay for capital investments such as acquisitions, new equipment / facilities and business expansion. This is relevant to UniMoose, as the CEO plans to expand and diversify the functions of her business to also bring in moose from nature preserves outside the state. Her options for long-term financing may be either debt or equity:

Debt examples:
- *Loans by banks, insurance companies, and finance companies* – These are typically for one to five years, although they may be renewable. There is an interest rate associated with these commitments, and there could be other covenants – conditions the company must meet – like maintaining a certain level of equity or restrictions on the sale of some of their

critical assets (like the facility where the moose live).

- *Capital leases* – This is a lease that is treated like a purchase, and will show up on UniMoose's balance sheet. For example, UniMoose could buy trucks that it intends to own at the end of the lease, but it needs to meet at least one of the following criteria:
  - o At the end of the lease, the organization either owns the item or can buy it for less than market value.
  - o The lease is for 75% or more of the economic life of the item.
  - o The present value of the lease payments is 90% or more of the cost of the asset.

Any lease that does not qualify as a capital lease is considered an operating lease. Operating leases currently appear only as expenses on the income statement, versus appearing on the balance sheet, but must be disclosed in the notes to the statements.

- *Bonds, notes, and debentures* – These are long-term "notes" or commitments sold to investors, like a promise on paper for five to thirty or more years. There is an interest rate involved (and it is fixed, but you could refinance the bond if the interest rate drops), and they can be sold to someone else.
- *Convertible debt* – This would not be relevant to UniMoose at this time because it involves stock prices, and UniMoose is not a public company. If it was, it could convert some of its bonds and debentures to the company's common stock price and, if the stock price rises, the lender can sell this and remove UniMoose's debt. Simply put, the debt is converted to equity that can be paid off.

Equity Examples: These were not applicable to UniMoose because the company does not have stock, and therefore cannot sell preferred or common stock. It would have applied to MooseTown.

- *Preferred stock* – normally does not have voting rights so no control is given up; usually pays a set dividend rate and has priority over the common stock for dividend payments and in case of liquidation.
- *Common stock* – normally has voting rights; does not necessarily pay dividends. If it does, the dividends may be tied to company performance. The Board of Directors sets the firm's dividend policy.

The CEO of UniMoose is inclined to keep her method for funding the company's growth strategy *simple*. She is leaning towards a debt example – borrowing money from a bank.

Before she makes her final decision, she needs to consider the **Time Value of UniMoose's Money**, to determine whether this long-term financing commitment will be in the best interest of the company. The value of money changes over time for many reasons. Money available at the present time is worth more than the same amount in the future due to its potential earning capacity. This core principle of finance holds that, provided money can earn interest, any amount of money is worth more the sooner it is received. Similar to yelling "Polo" after "Marco," you will hear people yell "compounding" after "interest" in the finance world. They are referring to the time value of money.

Since the CEO of UniMoose is leaning towards a debt option, she tests her plans in two ways:

1. **Weighted Average Cost of Capital (WACC)**, which is the average of the costs of financing through debt or equity, each of which is weighted proportionately. By taking a weighted average in this way, she can determine what the company should do with its capital based on how much interest it owes for each dollar it finances.

2. **Economic Value Added (EVA)**, which is the concept that a business unit must make more than the annual cost of the investment in the unit if it is to add value to its owners.

$$EVA = Net\ Operating\ Profit\ After\ Tax - (Capital\ Invested \times WACC)$$

Since the EVA value was positive in her calculation, she had justification to use debt as UniMoose's financing option.

Part 5: UniMoose begins to launch new products

UniMoose creates a capital budget, a subset of overall budgeting, for its larger projects and growth strategy. This is different from an expense budget in a few ways:

To Capitalize	To Expense
• Becomes an asset • Spreads cost over time • Realize tax benefits gradually	• Appears only on income statement as expense • Realize cost at once • Realize tax deduction immediately

Types of capital expenditure decisions include, but are not limited to:

- *Business expansion opportunities* like growing the tall grass that moose eat
- *New products or services* like microchip tracking devices
- *Equipment purchases* to herd the moose
- *Major IT projects* to store the moose's biometric information
- *Decisions for outsourcing* and buying leases
- *Acquisitions* of small-size competitors

The company is brimming with new talent and new ideas for growing the business. The CEO reminds the company that they have a limited capital budget and that they need to make smart choices about what projects they spend their allocated funds for the year on. The CEO communicates that she will make these decisions based on a few key levers: the project's **payback period** (the shorter the better), the **net present value** (NPR) and **internal rate of return** (IRR). The larger the NPR and IRR, the better for the company. She also committed to ranking the projects based on profitability, using a **profitability index**, and stated that she will not move forward with any project that falls below UniMoose's **hurdle rate**, the minimum rate that a company expects to earn when investing in a project.

STAGEGATE 1: The Cut-Offs (Payback, NPV, Hurdle Rate)
The ten new Vice Presidents of UniMoose submitted a project each, all aimed at advancing the CEO's vision for improving the transport and treatment of the North American moose that the company protects.
Each project submitted a **Payback Period**. This term is the time it takes to recover an investment. We use payback to

122

reject, not accept. This means a project can be rejected because it has too long of a payback period; a project should not move forward merely because its payback period is attractive (as there are other factors to be considered). In this case, any project that had a payback period of longer than 10 years was rejected by the CEO of UniMoose, because the strategic direction of the company might change in this length of time. This does not consider the total life of the investment. Quicker payback *may* mean less risk, but this depends on the project. As a general rule, technology projects normally should have a quick payback because technology evolves so quickly and often needs to be replaced as quickly.

Seven projects remained. Each Vice President outlined the **Net Present Value (NPV)** of their proposed project. This term refers to the value in the present of a sum of money, in contrast to some future value it will have when it has been invested at compound interest.

Any project with a negative NPV was rejected. They did not meet the company's **hurdle rate**: they delivered less value than the company needed and could make. Hence, the hurdle rate is also referred to as the company's required rate of return or target rate. In order for a project to be accepted, its internal rate of return must equal or exceed the hurdle rate.

Projects with a zero or positive NPV continued to be in the running for funding. A positive NPV indicated the project earns more than the hurdle rate and a zero NPV indicated the project has made the hurdle rate. As a result of these performance expectations, only four projects remained.

STAGEGATE 2: The Priority List (IRR & Profitability Index)

The four of ten remaining projects also reported their expected project **Internal Rate of Return (IRR)** – the ROI (return on investment). This is the "annualized effective compounded return rate," or rate of return that sets the net present value of all cash flows (both positive and negative) from the investment equal to zero. Think of the internal rate of return as the rate of growth a project is expected to generate.

Each of the four projects were then ranked on UniMoose's **Profitability Index (PI)**:

$$\frac{present\ value\ of\ cash\ inflows}{present\ value\ of\ cash\ outflows}$$

The higher the PI, the better the project. After this was complete, the CEO of UniMoose was able to allocate funding to the three projects with the highest ranking, and hoped to find capital for some of the remaining projects in the upcoming years.

Now the real work begins. UniMoose must execute these projects in order to expand the business and make a profit.

Part 6: One year later, UniMoose fails to make its numbers

Fast forward a year. Two of the three capital projects that the CEO of UniMoose had approved are failing to achieve even the **break-even in sales dollars**.

Unfortunately, the one project that was performing better than the break-even sales point was, to the dismay of the CEO, **not reaching its profit goals**. It would struggle to cover the losses of the two other failing projects.

The Chief Financial Officer at UniMoose determined that, in order to allow the three approved projects to live, the company would need to borrow more money, which it cannot afford to do.

The three projects are then shut down, and the company decided their ten VPs should leave. The CFO sold some of the company's assets on the Balance Sheet (mostly real estate) to pay back the bank loan, employee severance packages and other major expenses.

Part 7: UniMoose is Sold

Fast forward six months. The Board of Directors of UniMoose determine that the CEO was unfit to continue to in this position; they condemned her decisions to borrow a very large sum of money, approve three underperforming projects and her hesitation to shut down these projects earlier. As it is the Board of Directors' duty to hire and fire the CEO, the Board of UniMoose made the tough decision to terminate the current CEO and sell the company to MooseTown. To determine the value of the company before it received bids for an acquisition, the Board considered liquidity, leverage and profitability.

To determine the value of a private company like UniMoose, the Board uses the **Comparable Company Analysis (CCA)**, which involves searching for companies that are publicly traded that most closely resemble UniMoose. The process includes researching companies of the same industry (ideally, a direct competitor), life, growth rate and scale. Once an industry group has been established, averages of their valuations can be calculated to directionally delineate where the private company fits within its industry. The other method used to value a private company is the **Estimated Discounted Cash Flow**, where the discounted cash flow of similar companies in its peer group is calculated and applied to the UniMoose. *(For a publicly traded company* *like MooseTown*, the value is based on its share price multiplied by the number of shareholders.)

UniMoose was then sold to MooseTown.

What did we learn?
This chapter presented an overview of how to manage a company from a financial perspective. The scenarios that UniMoose experienced in its rise and fall are not uncommon in the real world. But the CEO of UniMoose survived this experience – she took the skills from operating this large private company to run a slightly smaller public company on the Fortune 500 list.

Am I ready to be a CEO?
Reading through this chapter is the first step in understanding, at the most basic level, what knowledge of corporate finance is required of future CEOs. Ideally, you would put this knowledge to work by volunteering for a finance-focused project in your early career and catapulting yourself into a role that gives you the opening to manage finances and make a monetary impact.

But financial experience is not the only factor that builds CEOs. I will discuss other elements in detail in the following chapters of this book.

It is still early – time is on your side, and you need to start somewhere. As Maya Angelou said, "nothing will work unless you do."

Chapter 7
Your Game Plan:
The Agenda Drivers

Ross Perot, an American business magnate, wisely said, "most people give up just when they are about to achieve success. They quit on the one-yard line. They give up at the last minute of the game, one foot from a winning touchdown." [lvii] Do not quit just yet. This chapter will advise you on how to build resilience and get what you want on your path to CEO. Business is a contact sport; if you are afraid to get hurt, you cannot win.

So, Who Are You?

In business, you are going to need to know how to convince people – about yourself and your ideas. In every situation you are in with other human beings, an underlying expectation for you to prove yourself exists.

An extensive study conducted by Harvard Business Review found that women are implicitly held to a higher standard than their male colleagues. [lviii] Proving yourself is harder for women, whether you are at the bottom of the food chain, or at the top. The truth is that when you walk into a room, the people in the room will subconsciously (and maybe consciously) wonder why you are in the room. What are *you* doing here?

In these ubiquitous situations, there are a number of methods you can adopt to develop your self-awareness on your journey to becoming a CEO. They are applicable to conversations, negotiations and crises. I advise you to relate these methods to situations you have found yourself in.

Establishing Trust

To effectively communicate with and influence people in our hyper-connected and transparent social business world requires being open and understanding. Trust builds relationship capital, which can be traded for support to sustain your success and overcome challenges. Building trust also creates a virtuous cycle of self-awareness. Credible and trustworthy leaders continually seek knowledge about their own self-awareness, like better understanding of their personal values or guiding principles. Being true to your values will breed consistency which, in turn, is a factor in increasing trust and credibility.

The constructive impact of being a trustworthy person is boundless. As a positive role model for your leaders, peers and employees, you have the potential to directly elevate an organization's culture and performance.

To establish trust in the workplace, I recommend three overriding objectives.

1. **Be Yourself**
a. **Self-disclose:** *I have started many of my meetings with "I am not an expert on this topic, and that is why I need your help."* This is the art of establishing a personal connection with the audience by revealing your own weaknesses. In one study, same-sex marriage advocates went door-to-door in a conservative California neighborhood in an attempt to influence voter opinions on the topic. Some of the canvassers were gay and, as part of the study design, they came out to their

listeners; and others were straight but discussed a gay friend or relative. The study found that gay canvassers had greater success in changing attitudes.[lix] Researchers believe the combination of personal contact and self-disclosure was key. Do not be afraid to be vulnerable, even with a tough audience.

b. **Share a narrative:** *I often use narrative, both personal and abstract, to motivate teams into aligning with my vision for a project or product.* Tell your audience anecdotes that apply to a situation you are in, to engage them in your line of thought and decision-making process and engage them emotionally. According to one 2015 study, listeners engaged in this way may be less likely to "resist counter-attitudinal messages within stories because the messages don't provoke much scrutiny."[lx]

2. Practice Emotional Intelligence

a. **Offer empathy:** *I always think twice before expressing empathy, to ensure it is received well by my audience.* The aim is to make your audience feel comfortable to discuss their thoughts. Not everyone appreciates emotional responses or physical contact (like a hug). In order to genuinely understand how someone else operates and react appropriately, you have to leave your ego at the door.

b. **Reciprocate:** One effective way to build trust is to tactically mirror emotions and language, such as by repeating the last one to three words a person said or paraphrasing their words to make them feel understood and safe. I worked with a former CEO who often stated, "said another way, ____, is that correct?" It often made his audience feel heard – but only reciprocate when you mean it.

3. **Be Collaborative**
a. **Deliver on your promises.** It is difficult to rebuild trust with individuals and groups of people when you have let them down. Avoid overpromising and under-delivering at all costs. If you cannot make a promise yet, "I don't know yet" is an acceptable answer, especially if you are able to communicate your next steps and your timeline for finding an answer.
b. **Manage surprises.** Stay closely connected with the people you interact with to update them on impending bad news. "Pre-selling," the art of warning your audience of something, gets the shock out of the way. Surprised people hardly make logical, fair decisions. Allowing time to think will usually allow your audience to arrive at the most logical decision, even if it is not fully aligned with what you are requesting.

I worked with a former CEO who directly established trust better than anyone else I have worked with. He had this keen sense that allowed him to sense buried emotions. He was so good at establishing trust – being his best, collaborative, emotionally intelligent-self – that employees across the company would ask him for advice, even when it worked against them. "Going to Todd" became a thing to do if you needed someone to confide in. After I mustered the courage to ask him directly, "How do you build trust so consistently and effortlessly?" he taught me what I have written about here.

Establishing Trust, **Paying Attention to Body Language**, Changing Conversation, Anticipating Criticism, Being Aware of your Biases.

Paying Attention to Body Language

Whether it is a business or personal interaction, multiple studies show that as much as 50% to 90% of communication is non-verbal. This means the "text-or-email-only" method relays less than half of the intended message which, in turn, causes misunderstandings. Yet the world sends over eight billion texts per day, and businesses encourage chat or text-only work environments as Gen-Y enters the workforce. My concern is not misinterpretation; it is the loss of our ability to understand and use body language to our advantage, especially in the workplace.

Understanding your baseline, and that of those around you, should be your first step. Skipping this often leads to misinterpretation. A baseline stance is a person's body language when the person is under no pressure. To arrive at a baseline, you may want to ask straightforward, softball questions. These are questions your counterpart is familiar with and has the answers to, so you can observe them in their most relaxed and honest state.

A former CEO I worked closely with was able to sense changes in body language better than those beautiful-mind detectives featured in televised crime shows. He did this by paying attention to micro-expressions. Take, for instance, the time I presented to the Board of Directors of a multi-billion dollar company, and asked him for feedback on my performance. I was nervous, because I was one of the first employees who was not a senior leader to present and I was seeking approval on a topic that could change the course of the company for the next century. His response was, "Oh, didn't listen to a word you said." I immediately freaked out internally – was it because he chose to be incompetent or because my presentation was genuinely boring? He saw this

131

reaction in my eyes and cut it off. He then jumped quickly to a mental list of body language changes and micro-expressions that more than a dozen directors in the room exhibited, in reaction to specific topics within my presentation. I was taken back. How could he have noticed all of this, all at once? He revealed it gets easier to do when you are able to first understand the "baseline" of those in the room – any change to this is jarring to him now, with practice.

Over my time working with him, he continued to educate me on baselines. One time, I watched him speak to one of his long-time employees in his office.

Him: How's it going?
Them [in a slightly higher pitch of voice]: It's good.
Him: That bad, huh?
Them: Yeah, in fact⋯ [30 minute personal conversation].

Again, I was absolutely floored. He picked up on something I, and most of the world, would have ignored. Flabbergasted, and after 30 minutes, I asked him, "HOW?" He told me that the easiest way to facilitate an effective read of someone's body language is to let them speak more than you do.

You may also be wondering how to catch someone when they are lying. Based on a number of scientific studies and accounts of behavioral experts, here are some of the things to watch out for in other people *and* yourself:

- The person may change their head position quickly, breathe more rapidly or shuffle their feet, out of higher alertness and anxiety
- The person stands very still and blinks less to compensate for their anxiety

- The person may subconsciously touch or cover their mouth because of a lack of confidence in their words
- The person tends to instinctively cover vulnerable body parts due to a heightened sense of guilt and awareness
- The person may stumble on their words, or repeat words or phrases and provide unwanted detail in order to convince themselves of a lie

On your journey to CEO, you will need to be cognizant of your body language and the body language of those around you. Here are some of the cues you need to be aware of, while you are evaluating others:

Eyes.
- **Acute Observations.** Watch your counterpart's cues, without being too shifty or obvious. If you have observed their baseline, you will notice signs of engagement, disengagement and tension, which will be apparent in their body language. Engagement actions, like head nods, forward leans and eye contact, point out interest and agreement. Disengagement actions, like leaning back, frowning and looking away, indicate that the individual is dispassionate, aggravated, apprehensive or sometimes bored. Additionally, tension cues like face-touching, firmly crossed ankles and a higher vocal pitch are signs of disapproval.
- **Eye contact.** The eyes are the most powerful part of our body language, and can express everything from happiness to annoyance, interest to pain. Frequent eye contact is interpreted as honesty and forthrightness. Staring is interpreted as aggression. These are obvious statements, but we forget that we have the power to be more intentional about our expressions.

Face.
- **Facial expression.** A critical message conveyed with a smile will have a totally different impact than one delivered with an angry face.
- **Smiling.** During a conversation, and especially during a mediation, keep the tone in the room warm, light and airy. Simply smiling from time to time does exactly that for you without adjusting the thermostat or opening a window. Even though you must always assume that your counterpart in the negotiation is not your friend, and will not be involved in the next conversation on the topic, smiling could change the tone of a mediation.
- **Head nodding.** A common negotiating tactic is to look your counterpart in the eye and nod your head, even in the face of disagreement and criticism. This nonverbal gesture reduces tension and leads to alignment. Beware of the instances when your counterpart is nodding their head but actually does not understand what is going on.

Hands & Feet.
- **Handshake.** Shaking hands at the beginning and end of an interaction signals openness or goodwill. In the business world, palm-to-palm contact is important for sincerity.
- **Hand-to-face.** Even when your eyes and facial expressions are genuine, hand-to-face movements such as holding the chin or scratching the face shows concern or lack of conviction. If a person is covering their mouth while telling you something, they may be lying.
- **Hand positions.** Your hands can indicate when you are anxious or stressed. In a conversation, hands should mirror confidence and serenity. If you clasp or fidget

with your hands, your counterpart will know that you are worried and will try to take advantage.

- **Feet.** Your feet can talk for you, and a number of scientists have proven this. For example, Professor Geoffrey Beattie, Head of School and Dean of Psychological Sciences at the University of Manchester, and research by shoemakers like Jeffery West, suggest that if a man is nervous, he will show his feelings by increasing his foot movement. Women however, do the opposite, and keep their feet still if they are nervous. The research states that "Alpha" males and females have a low level of leg and foot movement because they like to dominate and control the conversation and the same goes for their body. Extroverts do likewise but for different reasons, while shy people have frequent movements.

Body.
- **Posture.** If you are trying to appear dominant or authoritative, stand erect with shoulders back. A slumped position usually indicates insecurity, guilt or weakness.
- **Relaxedness.** In situations of conflict, you will benefit from a relaxed body position, especially in reaction to tension. This, along with a calm tenor of voice and non-violent words, will build trust and credibility with your counterparts.
- **Arms and legs position**. Folded arms or crossed legs, perhaps turning away slightly, indicates a lack of interest and detachment. Uncrossed arms and legs may be a sign of acceptance of your position or terms.
- **Space occupied.** Some people stand up and move around to be more dominant or threatening. Even while sitting, you can stretch your legs to occupy more space.

Standing while talking on the phone will make your voice sound more urgent, but pacing could make your tone sound unstable.

- **Micro-expressions and gesture collections.** Non-verbal signals generally come about in a collection of (often three) gestures. These are a set of any of the movements and actions above that emphasize a certain point of view. For example, shifty eyes, twitching feet and tensed hands are signs of anxiety and discomfort.
- **Mirroring.** Most people feel more comfortable and open with people in a similar position to themselves. An example would be sitting down to meet with a key vendor, rather than standing to deliver demands. Good managers practice this one to address personnel issues.

Establishing Trust, Paying Attention to Body Language, **Changing Conversation**, Anticipating Criticism, Being Aware of your Biases.

Changing the Conversation

On your path to becoming a CEO, you will need to communicate who you are and share your ideas in an effective way, almost every day. You need to convince a room full of executives with a separate agenda to drive yours, using their resources and time.

For many years, I resorted to talking louder and faster as a method for selling something. *This method never worked.* I quickly learned that volume or pitch of a voice, or the speed of a conversation, are not the most effective tools for communication. My main takeaway that I want to share with you is that the act of changing a conversation will give you power to control it. With control of a conversation, you will

136

be in a better place to effectively represent who you are and what you would like to share.

From my experience observing CEOs from the Chief of Staff vantage point, there are three levers for changing conversations.

Revealing the Truth

By speaking. Sometimes pointing out the elephant in the room will change a conversation and leave it in your control. I worked for a CEO who used this method as a means of driving his agenda. He was extremely sensitive about wasting resources and was hyper-alert when one of his team members asked for more time (days, not hours) than what would be typically allowed for the project at hand. In one situation, the team member had a slew of valid reasons – delays here, a lack of other resources there, and special circumstances that drove their need for more allotted time. The CEO addressed this head on, digging into the truth; he began logically and practically listing the tasks that needed to be completed and billed a fair timeline to each task. At the end of this, he exclaimed, "···so that adds up to about three hours." He had exposed the truth that if they were being productive, they would need hours, not days.

By remaining quiet. Sometimes, you can anticipate a change in conversation in your favor – all you need to do is remain respectful and strong in the moment the truth is set free. When I was in my Chief of Staff role and sat in on executive team meetings, I witnessed colleagues lose control of driving their own agenda because they did not stay quiet. One of the golden rules I learned, by watching the downfall of some pitches, was to "drop the mic and leave" when you get something even slightly resembling agreement. You see a head nod? Thank the room and *leave*. This was

137

unfortunately not what one of my colleagues did in the room, and he paid for it. He came in to present an initiative that received approval, but then lingered to discuss his other triumphs – one did not sit well with this audience, and he lost them. The CEO then retorted, "Sounds like there are a few things you need to work through."

A Form of Entertainment

The Ridiculous Distraction. Sometimes, you can change the conversation by distracting your audience. Donald Trump, during his presidential campaign, constantly redirected attention while his administration covered up a narrative. For example, one day Trump quietly settled a fraud lawsuit and avoided further prosecution from a class action suit. He tweeted once about the settlement and then published a series of tweets about Hamilton ten minutes later, which redirected attention.

The Culture Check. Sometimes, you can influence a conversation to drive your agenda by drawing your audience in with a cultural reference. It is a method that is difficult to execute, so it requires you to be very knowledgeable and practice. This is because cultural references evolve so quickly that it is hard to recall some of them accurately, and most people will not be in tune with the cultural references you are most familiar with. The experts, politicians, have shown they can make it work. For those who want to practice, here is an example from 1984: in the Democratic primaries, Walter Mondale suggested his rival Gary Hart did not have any substance by quoting a Wendy's fast food commercial that was popular at the time: "Where's the beef?"[lxi] After this, Mondale owned the audience's attention.

The Curve-Ball

The Tactical Retort. Sometimes, you can use ruthless or curt responses to throw your opponent off guard. Contrary to popular belief, this requires planning ahead, in order to ensure you do not say or do something that is not aligned with your or your institution's values. This has been done many times in the political sphere. In 1980, President Jimmy Carter was running against Ronald Reagan, and Carter may have crossed the line by overusing the same attack. Reagan used a little verbal Jiu-Jitsu by chortling, "Well, there you go again."[lxii]

A former CEO I worked with used to do this to drive his agenda. In one instance, I was passionately discussing a topic with him, in an attempt to get resources for a project. His jovial response to my attempt was, "You get so worked up so easily." He threw me off. Then he got me to do some of *his* homework, and drive his agenda.

The Tactical Switch. Sometimes, you can take your counterpart's exact words and use them to turn everything against them. Politicians do this often. In 1984, Reagan was running for re-election at age 73. When this surfaced in a debate, he stated, "I will not make age an issue of this campaign. I am not going to exploit, for political purposes, my opponent's youth and inexperience." His tactical switch gave him control over the conversation, for him to promote his agenda.

Using the truth, a form of entertainment or a curve-ball are key methods for changing, controlling and shaping conversations. These methods can be deployed in almost any conversation to convince people of your abilities or your ideas. When you use these tactics, keep your focus on your end goal or message, or you risk causing distraction from your main message.

Establishing Trust, Paying Attention to Body Language, Changing Conversation, **Anticipating Criticism**, Being Aware of your Biases.

Anticipating Criticism

Driving your agenda involves more than pushing forward. It also involves being prepared when someone pushes back. To prepare for situations like these, it is important to learn to anticipate criticism and be hyper-aware of your biases. As CEO, you will encounter bad news weekly from lawyers, your finance team, your security and your Human Resources team. Defensiveness is rarely seen as a desirable leadership quality. Good leaders will accept their faults without explanations or excuses, and discuss next steps and timeline instead. Good leaders may defend their team members in a blame game or when one of them is being unfairly accused.

A future CEO should be prepared for this.

You will not always have the luxury of being in control of the conversation, or the opportunity to seize control of the situation. In circumstances where you are *forced* to react, you will *need* resilience.

Steve Jobs, who encountered plenty of workplace hostility, employed a particular resilience strategy:[lxiii]

1. Anticipate criticisms of your stance
2. Do not react immediately
3. Give a broad opening line that feels favorable to the accuser, but qualified

4. Answer the question you want asked
5. Acknowledge the fallibility of you and your team, and then support both

Anticipating and reacting to criticism requires a strong sense of resilience and fearlessness. Ultimate Fighting Champion (UFC) and Mixed Martial Arts (MMA) fighter, Alexis Davis, taught me a lesson about resilience when I realized she is not afraid of anyone. Alexis is not afraid of larger men who have fought her or more powerful men who have attempted to fight her.

Alexis is from the same metro-area in Canada that a CEO I worked for (Tim Condon) is from. Tim, who also practices Brazilian Jiu Jitsu, once invited Alexis to feature in his keynote at a leadership conference, and to fight him on stage, in front of the entire company. His aim was to be humbled by an expert – a woman who is much stronger than he is. As Tim's Chief of Staff at the time, I must admit that I was concerned. Tim was a white belt and Alexis had more than one black belt. I recall emailing the organizers of the conference multiple times about sourcing thicker floor mats, and informing our Head of Security that this was actually going to happen. I also joked about CEO succession planning. On a different occasion, Tim engaged in a battle of wits with her, knowing he could not trump her physically. Even in this situation, Alexis quickly disarmed him, mid-sentence, when she said, "you talk a lot for a white belt." She beat him at his own game.

Each individual will have their own preferred method of anticipating and reacting to criticism. Here are a few things to ask yourself, to enable your journey to CEO:

• Are you wary of potential illusions of comfort that your circumstances may create? Ask for feedback and even for bad news as often as you can.

- Are you listening to your audience to understand or to react? Aim to listen more than you speak.
- Are you considered a trustworthy person? Understand what you can do to establish trust with the people around you.
- Are you prone to irrational behavior when you are surprised? Stop your first reaction, and ask for time to think about the feedback you have received.
- Are you appreciative of feedback? Saying, "Thank you, I appreciate you taking time to talk about this with me," will change the way you receive feedback in the future.
- Are you open to changing, based on feedback? Ask for time to revisit the topic. When you are ready, ask clarifying questions and share your perspective, to receive more feedback.

In fact, despite all of the lessons and advice in this book, you probably are not fit to be a future CEO.

That was a test. How would you react to a claim like that?

Establishing Trust, Changing Conversation, Paying Attention to Body Language, Anticipating Criticism, **Being Aware of your Biases** and Dispelling Stereotypes about Women.

Being Aware of Your Biases

Another crucial skill for driving your agenda to enable your path to CEO is being aware of your biases. In the business world, you trade the currency of credibility. If you cannot be trusted — if you lie, fall short of promises or act unfairly — you are generally less likely to operate as or become an effective leader. Subconscious biases unintentionally erode credibility, and even the most well-intentioned people are not free from these biases.

The list of subconscious biases below have the potential to jeopardize the brand you have built for yourself and the work you do. They are worth understanding in depth, in order to determine if you could identify and resolve them when they creep up on you.

Conservatism Bias. This bias leads people to believe that pre-existing information takes precedence over new information. Sound familiar? For example, a study presented employees with a company with two pieces of information – one much more familiar to the audience than the other; 99% of people weighted the information that is easy to understand as more important.

Allowing conservatism bias to impact your decision making process could severely decrease your credibility.

Fundamental Attribution Error. This is the tendency to attribute situational behavior to a person's fixed personality. As a manager, you may often attribute poor work performance of an employee to lethargy and apathy. You would be failing to consider other explanations, especially those pointing to the manager herself or the external environment. As a result, you may lose key Members of your team or create a hostile and unforgiving work environment that would discredit your ability to lead people and a business.

The Decoy Effect. This is a notorious CFO tactic. She will present the CEO with two viable options and one faulty one. This is a tactic to make the second option feel more palatable to you. Businesses probably use this bias against you already. For example, Apple uses pricing options on their products to make you choose the one they would like to sell, even if this not the best financial decision for you; the iPod Touch positions the pricing of the 16GB and 64GB options as price decoys, so users will go for the 32GB version, and pay $70 extra for the upgrade.

The Halo and Horn Effects. The Halo Effect is a common sales tactic and occurs when someone creates a strong first impression and that impression sticks. The Horn Effect is the exact opposite – it allows for a single negative trait to unduly influence the perception of other traits. For example, you are more likely to assume that someone on your team is a low performer if they are a casual dresser, despite the lack of a scientifically proven relationship between performance and dress code. Again, you could lose strong performers and future leaders on your team if you suffer from this bias. Your team's success is a key part of your success as a future CEO.

Confirmation Bias. This is the tendency to embrace new information as affirming pre-existing beliefs and to ignore evidence that does not. This psychological phenomenon is becoming more apparent in new social channels, like Facebook. Unlike Twitter, or real life, where interaction with those who disagree with you on political matters is an inevitability, Facebook users can block, mute or unfriend any outlet or person that is not part of their current worldview.

I saw the prevalence of this bias destroy a number of my colleagues' business projects. This occurred when they chose to ignore feedback that was not positive or financial projections that did not tilt in their favor. Their work lost the company millions of dollars in some cases, as well as the time and effort of their teams.

The Ostrich Effect. This is a direct reference to the fact that ostriches, when scared, literally bury their heads in the ground. This effect describes our tendency to hide from impending problems and lie to ourselves. During the financial crisis in 2008, many companies were blamed for ignoring the macroeconomic signs and even direct warnings from the Institute of International Finance (IIF). These warnings called for the need to make drastic, albeit inconvenient, changes at banks and other corporate goliaths – changes that could have cost billions of dollars.

The Bandwagon Effect. This effect is the tendency to do what everyone else is doing – in stock markets, clothing trends, sports fandom and even board room decisions. During the dotcom bubble of the late 1990s, dozens of tech startups emerged that had no viable business plans, no products or services ready to bring to market and in many cases nothing more than a name. Despite lacking in vision and scope, these companies attracted millions of dollars in investment. And while this bias made thousands of people millionaires, it could jeopardize your path to CEO.

If your preference is to hop on the bandwagon, you assume the risk of surrendering your opportunity to be unique. Uniqueness might even be the most influential factor in creating future CEOs, and I will discuss this in detail in Chapter 9.

Affect Heuristic. This effect allows people to make decisions quickly by allowing their current emotions to influence their decisions. Interestingly, attitudes toward climate change, nuclear power and consumer judgments (the zero-price effect) have been shown to be affected by this heuristic.[lxiv]

Unfortunately, in the workplace, passion is often mistaken for emotion without thought, and our society assumes that women suffer from affect heuristic more than men. During Secretary of State Hillary Clinton's campaign trail, the media pounced on her for tearing up once, despite her unswerving, controlled demeanor. Similarly, former Yahoo

CEO Carol Bartz is frequently cited for her "salty language," which has been used as evidence that she is "emotional" and a "loose cannon."[lxv] The Harvard Business Review found that based on one thousand 360-degree feedback reports on female executives, when women fervently sell an idea or argue against the consensus, for example, a male colleague or manager's response was often along the lines of, "she was too hyped up" and "she was emotional." The women themselves say they were simply advancing their cause or expressing an opinion, albeit passionately.[lxvi] Napoleon Hill, a best selling American self-help author, once said that "obsessed is just a word the lazy use to describe the dedicated."

Bias Blind Spot. This is the phenomenon that you are more susceptible to develop bias blind spots if you believe you do not have any, and tend to see biases in other people but not in yourself. A study conducted by Carnegie Mellon found that only one adult out of 661 said that they are more biased than the average person, when in fact, many participants belonged in that category.

As you digest this section, remind yourself to continue to be aware of the bias blindspot. Your intelligence, cognitive ability, decision-making ability, self-esteem, self-presentation and general personality traits are found to be independent characteristics that not related to the bias blind spot, and therefore can negatively impact you in your journey to the top.[lxvii]

What Does Success Look Like?
Driving your agenda throughout your journey is a balancing act of thoughtfully utilizing the five tools discussed above – establishing trust, paying attention to body language, changing conversation, anticipating criticism and being

aware of your biases. Your traits are most evident in how you communicate.

You maintain factual accuracy and clarify everything. You fully understand the tone of the conversation and are not afraid to ask dumb questions. (Preface it with, "Can I ask you a dumb question?") You give credit to the experts. You spend your time crafting a message that the other person wants to hear, as long as it is true. Above all, you do not lie.

You reveal the right amount of personal information. You are comfortable with vulnerability. You know what your counterpart wants to hear but you keep it brief and specific, because most people will disengage if content is not personally valuable to them. The personal level does not have to be deep. It just has to exist.

You read body language while adjusting your own. You see non-verbal cues and you hear shifts in tone. You calculate before you react, and you allow your counterpart to react fully before you calculate. Above all, you listen.

You engage through active listening and questions. You change the way you ask questions. You avoid questions that test your counterpart's ability to understand you, like "Do you know what I mean?" Instead, you offer safety, control and being right by placing the emphasis on yourself. You ask, "Am I explaining this well?" or "Stop me if I am wrong." You invite your counterpart into the conversation. Above all, you listen to understand, not to respond.

You improve your ability to convince people – of yourself and your ideas.

CEOs are not created with just resume builders and agenda-driving traits. You will need support boosters, a unique brand and the answers to some tough decisions as you continue your journey. Read on.

Chapter 8
Your Game Plan:
The Support Boosters

As you practice driving your agenda, you need supporters in your community to back you up. As a united force, you and other women would be more prepared to fight gender biases and combat gender stereotypes.

Finding Your Support Network

One of my mentors once told me, "You are the average of the five people you associate with most in your career. So, pick wisely and don't underestimate the negative effects that one person can have on your upward trajectory." From this conversation, I learned that if someone is not boosting you to where you want to go, they are likely making you weaker, or less equipped to succeed.

Remember two things as you think about building your support network – there is power in the pack, and the pack will be stronger once you realize your strengths and bring them to the table.

Research in the 2019 Harvard Business Review shows that women need two support networks, while men require one to succeed in the same way.[lxviii] The study identifies that both women and men profit from engaging with a well-connected, diverse (in demography, geography and psychography) peer network. Women, however, need that extra inner circle of close female connections and champions to make them more likely to climb to executive roles with more compensation and authority.

Viviane Ford, my friend and the Vice President of an autonomous vehicle start-up in Silicon Valley taught me this before HBR did. Viv was so impressive at maintaining two support networks, and engaging with them in different ways, that, for years, she served as my plus-one at work events. I once invited her to speak to my team about her ability to network. She called into this meeting on her phone, while she was walking three miles to her next "pack" event. Viv has many circles – of friends, colleagues, influencers, mentors and every other kind of group of people you can imagine; and she's good at mobilizing all of these groups around causes that are important to her. She takes the "working" out of "networking," and this is a trait that is valued tremendously by her inner circle of female friends.

Identify the right mentors and sponsors early. While mentors offer encouragement and advice, and are most influential at an earlier career stage, sponsors take a hands-on role in managing career moves and promoting executives as potential CEOs. Mentors will find themselves pushing someone up; sponsors will exert a force that resembles a hard pull. Whether that sponsor is a previous CEO, another senior executive, Board Member, or external CEO, they are crucial support for elevating women to senior leadership positions. But sponsors have little incentive to say your name in public if you have not built a strong brand. A large part of mentorship is understanding what not to look for. As you selectively choose your mentors and decide what kind of a mentor you want to be, here are the key takeaways:

1. **Person > Position**: You or your mentor will change titles and companies through your engagement. Look for the *person* in your mentor, not the position they hold.

2. **Flexibility > Expectation:** Be flexible with the scope of the opportunity and the level of attention you receive. After all, their efforts are voluntary. Try to find ways to give more than you take.
3. **Unconventional > Standard:** Search outside your comfort zone as well as right beside you for someone who can develop you by offering many different perspectives.
4. **Journey > Destination:** Avoid asking for a CEO roadmap, but ask for advice on how to navigate situations. Remember that mentorship is not a life vest.

I have been fortunate enough to have incredible mentors. Some of them, like the CEOs I worked with and the women I have featured in this book, were chosen intentionally. Wherever I have worked, I have deliberately sought female role models. At a company where I spent most of my early career, a number of women emerged as my mentors and sponsors. I thoroughly appreciate that the head of the legal department occasionally sent me motivational texts and advice from her career, and other senior leaders made time during their busy schedules to give me career advice.

Through my workplace and additional networking, I met a number of mentors who have continued to guide me. Patti Lee, one of my performance coaches, first began advising me on how to develop a personal, unique brand, and then continued to send me reminders that I *am* a future CEO. Jennifer Botterill, a four-time Olympic medalist and another one of my performance coaches, consistently reminds me of the "why not me?" mindset. Alexis Davis, an Ultimate Fighting Champion, assured me that I should not care about what others think, and that sometimes, I will need to fight myself to get to where I deserve to be.

Along my journey, I also found mentors unexpectedly in other people. Shahareen Ghouse, my mother and a life-long teacher, encouraged me to move 10,000 miles away from home to pursue my dreams. My sister, Shamira Ghouse, and my best friend Arushka Theagarajah played an integral role in encouraging a positive outlook on my career, even in the most difficult of times.

Laura Furstenthal, a managing partner at McKinsey, taught me that there is no traffic on the extra mile. I cannot name any managing partners of multi-national, multi-billion dollar corporations who would travel out of their way to spend time with me. Laura did. Despite her exceptionally busy work, travel and family schedule, she carved out time in her day to meet me to discuss women in the workplace. Her actions inspired me to pay it forward in many ways, and I hope her actions will inspire you too.

Supporting Other Women

Women are meant for great things, and you can play an active role in mentoring those around you. As I shared in *Chapter 2*, your legacy will be stronger when it is geared toward more than just your success. Laura Furstenthal and Laura Zeigler, who shared their powerful intended legacies, showed me that. There are a number of compelling reasons to support women in your community.

The world needs to be exposed more to the female perspective and voice. Chapter 3 dived deep into the force fields in your environment that serve as a challenge for women in Hollywood and in the business world. According to the BBC, science gear, military equipment, smart phones, office-space temperatures sports gear and car crash dummies are mainly tested on and built for ease of use among males. For example, the US government used the average 50th percentile male body as a dummy for car crash testing only; according to a study by the University of

Virginia, this increased the risk of injury by 71% for female drivers involved in crashes.[lxix] In March 2019, NASA cancelled an all-female spacewalk because the spacesuits it makes would not fit the female astronauts. NASA could not configure more than one medium size space suit, and does not make them in the small size. The outrage this caused in support of gender equity led to the introduction of female crash test dummies in 2012 and a movement to reschedule the all-female NASA spacewalk.

Women are a key driver of current and future economic growth. According to the CEO of the Centre for Sustainability and Gender Economics, the annual GDP in Australia would increase by $180 billion, representing a 13% growth rate, if women worked full-time. If women's participation in the workplace matched that of men, ASEAN countries could add US $1.2 trillion of GDP to their economies, 30% more than now. By advancing women's equality in the workplace, Canada could add $150 billion to GDP by 2026.[lxx] One McKinsey report estimates that if women played the same role in labor markets as men, as much as $28 trillion, or 26%, could be added to global annual GDP by 2025.[lxxi]

Women are driven by achieving business results and making a positive impact. Harvard Business Review interviewed dozens of female CEOs and found that more than two-thirds assessed said they were inspired by a sense of purpose and believed that the company could have a positive impact on its community, its employees or the world around them. [lxxii] A *Catalyst* report found that companies with the largest representation of women in their management teams experienced healthier financial performance than companies with the lowest representation – a 35% higher return on equity and a 34% higher return for shareholders.[lxxiii] Credit Suisse Research Institute reported similar findings – companies with female CEOs showed a 19% higher return on equity and a 9% higher dividend payout.

Women are making a measurable impact on innovation. A 2017 study found that "companies with the greatest gender diversity (8 out of every 20 managers were female) generated about 34% of their revenues from innovative products and services in the most recent three-year period."[lxxiv]

Along your journey to CEO, I encourage you to freeze any signs of envy. I define jealousy as wanting something that someone else has, and envy as wanting something someone else has *and* wishing that the other person did not have it. Envy is more malicious than jealousy. The world needs more female supporters and mentors. In a keynote speech, Madeline Albright once said, "There's a special place in hell for women who don't support other women." A study by L'Oréal Foundation that surveyed 5,000 people across Europe also found that, when asked what impeded women's rise to the top, 45% of women believed that men blocked women's progression, and 44% of them (compared with 37% of men) said there was a problem in the support management provided for women.[lxxv] The world, and women in particular, don't need more envy.

To make sure you are supporting those around you, test yourself. If you have attended any ethics seminar or leadership development class on making the right decisions, you would have heard the "Loved One" test. In the 1980s, Harvard Law School placed an ethics course in their curriculum which generated more than a modest amount of chuckles. The first question the instructor would raise to the class would be, "what is the barometer you use for making ethical decisions?" The Loved-One test is the equivalent of asking yourself, "Would I be ashamed of telling my mother what I did?" If the answer is ever yes, then you know you are in the wrong.

If every aspect of your job search process were visible to your mother, would she be proud? If your mother heard your list of excuses for not pursuing the career path to CEO, would she be satisfied? If your mother saw you turn down an opportunity to mentor a young girl, would she be pleased?

How can you support women on your path to CEO?

Empowered women empower other women. Ask yourself, "How can I be a mentor and create women-empowered workplaces?" Or, "how can I change gender-biased industries like Hollywood to change the future?" Or, "how can I use my time to ensure women do not have to wait until 2059 to be paid as much as men?" There are many factors that limit women from making it to CEO. Thus, there are many elements of the issue to address.

In the business world, for example, you can start by building female-friendly workplaces by:

- *Offering flexibility.* According to Werk, a business that supports workplace flexibility for individuals and companies, 70% of women who dropped out of the workplace said that they would still be working if they had been given flexibility. According to the Harvard Business Review, employees who are given the autonomy to work flexibly are happier, more productive and less likely to quit.
- *Encouraging female role models:* Actively identifying female successes, shouting out their achievements, proving more training and support, enabling mentor-

154

mentee relationships and actively encouraging women to apply for leadership roles will help them with their self-belief. Seeing more female role models in senior positions will create a more positive support network and in turn encourage more young women to apply to join the workforce.

- *Managing bias:* Actively encouraging an open dialogue and discussion in the workplace around bias and mistreatment will support more women to be employed, retained and empowered.

Beyond your desk job, you can make an impact in young girls in your community as well, by:

- *Combating bullying and oppression.* Unfortunately, only 19% of women have a positive association with the expression "like a girl." The #LikeAGirl social experiment in 2015 recruited women, men, boys and pre-pubescent girls and asked them to show what it meant to run like a girl and throw like a girl. Young girls performed these actions confidently and proudly, while older women and men performed these actions in a self-deprecating and frivolous manner. And we also allow society to disparage everything that young girls admire. A BBC short story featured a strong young woman on video powerfully stating:

> When we live in a world where we are taught to hate everything to do with teenage girls. We hate the books they read and the bands they like. Is there anything the world makes fun of more than One Direction and Twilight? We call them ditzy and bitchy, and when teenage boys are cruel to them, we say, "boys will be boys."[lxxvi]

- *Challenging young women to reach further and higher.* We hold little girls to standards of "perfect" when we should be encouraging them to reach "excellent" through imperfections and failures. In 1980, psychologist Carol Dweck looked at how intelligent fifth graders coped with a challenging assignment. She discovered that bright girls were quicker to give up – the brighter, the faster they quit and more likely they were to quit. Boys, on the other hand, were energized by the challenge and were more likely to double their efforts.[lxxvii] Every graduating senior of elementary, middle school, high school, college and grad school should operate with the confidence levels that they are built to overcome challenges and reach the top.

Combating Gender Stereotypes Together

Women who combat standard stereotypes are often bucketed into new ones. Here are three prevalent stereotypes that women have endured over the past century, and the new stereotypes that are emerging.

Stereotype #1: Women have not developed the skills and demeanor required for the role.[lxxviii]

Many studies – by McKinsey, the Korn Ferry Institute, etc. – indicate society still believes that while women are skilled at role-specific tasks, they are not fit to manage people, lead or collaborate. A man, on the other hand, with identical qualifications and experience will be assumed to be able to lead well, delegate responsibly and effectively communicate with peers. This stretches beyond the business world into other disciplines as well. The L'Oréal Foundation surveyed 5,000 people across Europe on their views and perceptions of scientists. It found that 67% of Europeans think that women do not possess the required skill set in order to achieve high-level scientific positions (in the UK, the figure is 64%).[lxxix] In China, 93% believe that women do not possess the skills and demeanor to be scientists.

Unfortunately, when women break the mold and prove that they do, in fact, have the skills and the demeanor to excel at an opportunity, they are labeled as "conniving," "engineered," "angry," etc. For example, NBC's Ann Curry was told that she could not be a news reporter because women have "no news judgment," when she first started her career. When asked what irked her the most, she said, "The idea that a woman can only be successful because she somehow **connived** or **engineered** her rise – that she could not rise simply because she was too good to be denied."

Women who prove this stereotype false are presented with a fresh set of even more extreme stereotypes, from ice-queen to cheerleader. For example, Billie Blair, president and CEO of Change Strategists, stated that prominent women who are considered sincere and feminine are often labeled "**cheerleaders**." In fact, Blair recalls hearing a male client call former Alaska Governor Sarah Palin "a **cheerleader**, not a coach nor a quarterback," when Palin was running for Vice President. On the other extreme, Halley Bock, CEO of leadership and development training company Fierce, has encountered the ruthless "**ice queen**" neo-stereotype. Bock noted, "A woman who shows emotion in the workplace is often cast as **too fragile** or **unstable** to lead… A woman who shows no emotion and keeps it hyper-professional is **icy** and **unfeminine**. For many women, it can be a no-win situation."

Another good example dates back to 2008 during the presidential election when former First Lady Michelle Obama was condemned as an "**angry** black woman" while she was campaigning. While anger is a sign of status in men, society views it as a signal of incompetence in women. A

2008 series of studies by the Harvard Kennedy School's discovered that spectacles of anger from males in professional environments are considered to be reactions to peripheral situations, while the same from females are viewed as illustrations of character. Society believes men are provoked, while women are inherently prone to anger. Additionally, the study found that women who conveyed anger in work situations were observed as less competent and received lower wages, while the opposite was true for men.[lxxx]

Stereotype #2: Women do not have the dedication and work ethic to succeed in their careers.[lxxxi]

The historical model of men as the provider of a family or community is about to change. The pipeline of women entering college and then the workforce is strengthening. The number of women earning a bachelor's degree in business jumped from 9% in 1970 to 50% in 2000. Women today outnumber men in American colleges. In 1960, there were 1.6 males for every female graduating from a U.S. four-year college; by 2003, that had flipped to 1.35 females for every male.[lxxxii]

Even little girls are proving they have the work ethic to be successful. In fact, girls tend to have fewer behavioral issues than boys. These behavioral factors, after adjusting for family background, test scores and high school achievement, can essentially explain what was seen for the high school graduating class of 1992, according to the National Bureau of Economic Research, where females had an advantage in getting accepted to college. Similarly, teenage boys, both in the early 1980s and late 1990s, had a higher incidence of arrests and school suspensions than teenage girls.

Stereotype #3: Women make life choices that do not complement their work.[lxxxiii]

When a professional woman has a family, it is often assumed that she prioritizes her role as a mother over her career. This is, however, not the perception for fathers. In reality, 80% of women who plan to leave their company in the next two years intend to stay in the workforce – only 2% of women leave workforce to focus on family, versus 1% of men.[lxxxiv]

Unfortunately, when women choose to work over having children, they are labeled as masculine or single and lonely, and often face harsh judgments. While men get to be "bachelors," women are seen as **"spinsters"** and **"old maids."** In fact, when Janet Napolitano was nominated Secretary of Homeland Security, critics said her being single would allow her to "spend more time on the job."

The nuances of female stereotyping are important to understand as you build yourself to be a CEO. You will play an integral role in shaping what success looks like for women, and dispelling stereotypes that could form, by supporting and boosting other women.

You can make a difference. In the first year after the placement of the "Fearless Girl" statue on Wall Street and a gender-focused outreach, 152 companies added a female Board Member, and another 34 companies committed to adding at least one woman to their board in the near term.

Every woman should have said, at least once, "I want to be CEO"; the earlier this is vocalized, the stronger the voice becomes.

You could go on this journey on your own and bravely fight the invisible force fields that obstruct your ability to succeed. While I would respect anyone who chooses this path, it is unlikely to be the most effective way to move forward; the time commitment needed to proceed on your own may force you to give up time spent on other activities – potentially time traveling for leisure or spent with friends and family. Or, you could leverage the support of others who will help to boost you to where you want to go.

Chapter 9
The Cherry On Top

The difference between ordinary and extraordinary is that little "EXTRA." – Jimmy Johnson

Let us assume that you have the motivation to be CEO, the advanced financial acumen, all the traits that successful CEOs possess, the right mentors in place, a sense of value for your time and the unencumbered drive to fulfill your goals. You are still missing one final ingredient. It is the ability to package and market all of your strengths to your professional advantage. It is the ability to create a unique brand.

If your story does not inspire yourself, it is time to change it. In a 2017 assessment of more than 141 million LinkedIn Member profiles, the networking site found that gender stereotypes and tendencies are pervasive even in the way women present themselves as job candidates online. When looking at LinkedIn member data, they found men tend to skew their professional brands to highlight more senior-level experience, often removing junior-level roles altogether. Women are more likely to have shorter profile summaries. Additionally, in the U.S., women on average include 11% fewer skills than men on their LinkedIn profile, even those with similar occupations and experience levels.[lxxxv] Recruiters who hunt predominantly on LinkedIn use these lists because they are an effective summary that could easily match to a job description requirement. This means that women could be underselling themselves and, as a result, are approached less about bigger opportunities.

Regardless of how stained your past may be, your future is pretty spotless. As John F. Kennedy said, "the time to repair the roof is when the sun is shining." Why market yourself? Because we need to stop spending our lives *finding* ourselves when we can spend this time *creating* ourselves.

Unique, Just Like Everyone Else

Unique has become the new normal. It is how you get into the college of your choice. It is how you make friends. If you are not unique in the world today, you propel yourself into extinction.

While it is tempting to be general, you are more likely to leave your mark if your brand represents one unique quality. I learned this from the late Dr. John Briscoe, my favorite teacher at Harvard college. He gave me some of the best advice I will perhaps ever receive. In a one-on-one advisory session, he said, "Sabrina you are a jack-of-all-trades. You might think that's great. I see that as your flaw. Pick one thing, and be really good at it. If you remember me for anything, it better be this."

Initially, I was hurt. He thought I was flawed. But he inspired me to search for a better understanding of a unique quality my personal brand could be focused on. After working closely with CEOs, and engaging personal brand experts for business women, I will share my advice with you. Your personal brand is the cherry on top – it is what packages everything I have talked about so far.

How do I build my brand?

Take a step back. You will need to first understand your own value.

Your value isn't based on who you work for or your position at a job. It's based on what you're able to bring to the table. What do you do extremely well and who does it best serve?

In business, we invest in finding a target audience and a niche market for our products and services. It helps you narrow down the list of potential customers (or employers) who you can best help and who you are passionate about engaging with. Create a value proposition that speaks to what you do and who you help most. For example, sometime in your career you will hopefully say, "I help young women early in their careers to feel equipped on their path to becoming CEOs."

In order to effectively position your personal and unique brand in the workplace and in your community, you have to know what issues your environment is facing and how you could be a part of the solution. What does an organization stand to lose without you? That is where your value lies.

Now, branding. A brand is a collection of things – a symbol, design, name, sound, reputation, emotion, employees, tone and much more – that separates one thing from another. In the case of McDonald's, the golden arches separate the product from that of all other fast food restaurants.

Branding on a business level is common, but today branding is becoming just as important on a personal level. After all, you might work for a business that works with other businesses; but it's also people working with people and that's what makes business relationships valuable.

Take these steps: create a personal brand vision, define your audience and create online and office assets. This very closely resembles how businesses build their brands.

1. Create a personal brand vision

Businesses create vision and mission statements. Creating a personal brand begins much the same way.

Only you can determine how you want your life to unfold. You can't control every aspect of your life, but you can

163

create a long-term vision and develop steps to achieve that vision.

Your life's vision or goal should include how you see yourself in 10, 20 and even 50 years. What in life would make you happy? A family? A beach house? A challenging corporate job as CEO? There are no right or wrong answers.

My brand vision received a lift when a former manager told me I could be a CEO (remember that 65% of female CEOs say the primary reason for believing they could be CEO is that someone told them it was possible). It shaped the way I valued myself and my career; it even shaped the sentence I thought of after my name – "not your average future CEO."

Linking your brand to emotions will strengthen the way it is received. Humans have a desire to be understood. Shared emotions will often trump differences. For example, friendships can be built on common likes as well as dislikes. If your brand forms naturally, out of strong emotions, let it happen. This genuine form of brand-building is rare and valuable.

Laura Furstenthal, one of my mentors, has a strong brand that is built on genuine past experiences. When I asked her what her brand was, she said, "Servant leadership with a smile. Doing more listening than talking; caring more about the success of others than myself, which truly amplifies impact; always seeing the positive next step, no matter what the history."

I asked Laura where this admirable passion for her community stemmed from. She told me that although she was born and raised in the Bay Area, a student exchange to the Soviet Far East at the age of 15 left a huge impression on her. She saw propaganda at its height. She saw Boris Yeltsin speak to a warehouse full of laborers in Habarosk about how capitalism would bring a washing machine to every house and a car to every family. Meanwhile, she stayed with a family in a cinderblock apartment where three kids piled into a bedroom with their parents to give her the only other room. Once every two weeks, the kids and her got a single tiny square of butter as a special treat. Laura told me, "This experience taught me a lot about gratitude, about the importance of honest and values-driven leadership, and made me realize how self-reliant I could be."

If you are not ready to feel vulnerable, you will not build a strong brand vision for yourself.

2. Define your audience

Once you have your vision, it is time to determine who your target audience is. In the business world, most people sell products or services to a specific customer. For your personal brand, you will be selling your unique characteristics and the value you add to your target audience. In most cases, your audience will be your employers, your peers and, potentially, prospective mentors.

3. Create online and offline brand assets.

Your asset strategy should be simple, with the aim to address the questions and solve the problems that your target audience has.

In personal branding, assets are the things you own that will communicate your brand message to your target audience. Assets are things like your own website and blog, but they can also be things like your Twitter handle and your LinkedIn profile. Offline assets are things like business cards and or traditional newsletters that you send out.

- Social media – You could start with Facebook, which is an affirmation that you exist. Next, move on to Twitter and Instagram. Later in this section, I will discuss how the content you publish will shape your brand.

- Professional media – Start with LinkedIn, the biggest social network aimed at professionals. Your LinkedIn account is affirmation that you exist in the professional world, are employed now and have been employed in the past. It is not only a helpful place to look for opportunities beyond your current job, but it also shapes the way your colleagues in your current job see you. The extent to which you keep your profile up to date – the descriptions you have crafted for yourself and the content that you share – paint a picture of how engaged you are in your career development and growth.

- Personal website – Your personal website is the most important element of your brand strategy. This is because you own the content on your site and you control the platform. It is also because not everyone invests time in maintaining a website, unlike a Facebook or LinkedIn account. This will help you to stand out in a crowd of future leaders. (Obtain an exact match domain for your brand name, because people generally trust a website URL that matches your name as close as possible.) Beyond the content, the design and layout of the website is also a tool you could deploy to express yourself; designs evolve quickly, so be sure to explore other websites that resonate with you before you design yours.

- Personal Blog – A blog gives you an opportunity to present fresh, relevant content to your target audience. You could launch promotions, as well as link it to your social media, professional media and personal website. Once you are comfortable with managing a blog, expand this strategy by responding to your target audience in online forums, and linking your answers to your personal media and blog. This is a very similar strategy to that of product marketing teams, which create content for their audience in order to build trust and expertise, before suggesting they purchase their product.

- Hosting or attending events – Imagine if you became the connection point in an industry or marketplace for your target audience. Focus on bringing your online and offline supporters together to put a face, voice and body to your name using the skills mentioned in *Chapter 7*. Hosting an event will also give you the opportunity to interview industry influencers which, in turn, will strengthen your brand's credibility.

What happens after I build my brand?

First, practice living your brand through narratives. Patti Lee, my personal brand coach and an incredible mentor to women, reminded me that everyone learns how to tell stories – no one is born with this talent. She said:

> Who, what, when, where and why were the foundation for every good story. But it's the WHY that gives a story heart. A powerful story can transform communities and bring out the best in individuals. It can unveil ugly truths and compel even the most complacent to take action. Most of my bosses used to joke, "Don't the let the facts get in the way of a good story." They were kidding, of course, but the strength of a good story lies not in the accuracy of its facts but in its authenticity.

Patti has covered some of the biggest news in the country. Now she helps others get to the heart of their stories and personal brands so they can take charge of their future. In 2015, Patti started coaching startup founders on sharing brand stories and best practices of pitching to the press and potential investors. Patti has spent years researching effective communication techniques and the importance of knowing your audience. She believes getting to know your audience involves being active in your community.

To replace the five Ws, Patti encouraged me to focus on the AAA of storytelling. She taught me:

- Authenticity. Don't be afraid to show your genuine, authentic self. You know you are fascinating, so resist the urge to embellish details or falsify anecdotes (remember Brian Williams?). An audience can tell when a story doesn't ring true. If people don't trust your story's authenticity, it's difficult for them to create an emotional connection with your brand. The key is to get to the heart of your story. The experiences and details you share in your story reveal your values and beliefs. What drives your vision and fuels the difference you make? What is your *why*?
- Audience. Make a meaningful connection by tailoring your brand story to your audience. Who is part of this community and what connects you to them? Consider their interests, aspirations and cultural connections, and even the quirks you share in common. All of these can be the basis for emotional connection. Your story needs to show that you get it.
- Adversity. In developing your story, start with experiences that made you who you are and qualify you to serve your community. In documenting your career/life journey, include the missteps and transitions that formed you. It is tempting to shy away from these details but as Lisa Cron, author of Wired for Story, explains, "A story is how what happens affects someone who is trying to achieve what turns out to be a difficult

goal, and how he or she changes as a result." In your story, you are that someone. Where you are today is the result of having dealt with doubts, flaws, turning points and overcoming conflicts. Include examples of how you persevered in the face of uncertainty, adversity or risk.

One way to gain exposure is to get press coverage. There are a number of tools that make it easy to build connections with journalists, bloggers and moderators. Building these relationships and understanding what the press wants gives you the power to get free press.

Second, get testimonials and track your brand to build on your value and strengthen your brand.

Testimonials will help you to validate that your value and brand are unique. If you consistently deliver value to a workplace or your community, ask for this validation in writing or in a public forum. In the business-marketing world, this would be the equivalent of building a loyal network of brand ambassadors that drives organic support and demand in the future. Start by asking your professional network (even your existing employer) to give you a testimonial – request that they highlight and specify what you excel at and how they see you becoming a leader in your industry.

Once you have established your personal brand and you are investing time and effort to grow it, you will benefit from monitoring its growth and perception. This, again, is similar to how product marketing teams at corporations operate.

In fact, keeping tabs on your brand is necessary. Your personal brand revolves around your name. You must maintain control over your name if you want to gain recognition. Having intentional, strong and positive recognition can make it easier for your audience to discover you when they seek you out for information you have created online. Your online reputation might not determine whether you become a CEO, but there is more to lose if you are not protecting your name. Here are some ways to track your brand:

- **Typing your name into Google.** Here, you also have the opportunity to determine how your name appears in search rankings and on search engines like Google, Bing and social media.
- **Separate your name from others that share your name.** Tracking your name becomes more challenging when you have a common name and you could be confused for someone else. If this is the case for you, then you will need to find a more distinctive identifier for your online presence – for example, using a combination of your initials and a part of your name to create something that resembles a stage name.
- **Keep your content updated to see change over time.** If you search for the names of people with strong personal brands, you will notice that their personal websites and blogs appear high in the results. You will also see their social profiles. The linkage between accounts is a reminder to keep all active content current.
- **Consider removing extreme brand-damaging content** (for example, false information or unnecessarily inflammatory narratives of a situation) by contacting content owners, deleting social profiles or reaching out to the social network or reporting negative mentions if they break the rules on the site.

When you build your personal brand online, you might get negative responses to your posts. Don't correct people's feelings – if someone has made up their mind about you by criticizing you on a public forum online, there is little chance in convincing them otherwise online. Remember two things:

(1) this is one opinion of you, and (2) you shouldn't block yourself from constructive criticism. Not all feedback is unhelpful. In fact, some kinds of feedback could add value to your brand. If someone challenges your brand as a copy, you may want to make your brand more unique.

How will I use my personal brand on my path to becoming a CEO?

It will benefit you most in four situations:

Your Impending Interview

The oldest trick in the book is to "dress for the position you want, not the position you have." In one psychological experiment, participants were given a white laboratory coat to wear. Half of the participants were told it was a doctor's coat, half were told it was a painter's coat.[lxxxvi] Those who thought they were wearing the doctor's coat showed a heightened sense of attention. How a person feels about the clothes that they are wearing could affect the brain. What you wear also has the power to impact the behavior of those around you. Another experiment suggests that women who wore a sweater with a logo on it received a response rate (in the form of compliments or comments) of 52%, compared to non-logo sweater-wearing women, whose response rate was only 13%.[lxxxvii]

Women place more emphasis on dressing for the part than men do. In one Harvard Business Review study, 53% of women interviewed said that they felt like what they wore in the workplace was a vital factor in professional success, while only 37% of the men believed work opportunities or executive presence and attire were linked.[lxxxviii] This phenomenon can be attributed partly to unfortunate gender-specific preferences that still exist in our work culture.

Women are less likely to embrace gray hair in corporate America.[lxxxix] Women recognize this and have reacted – in 1950, 7% of women dyed their hair to get rid of their gray hair; in 2012, the number was closer to 95%, in some locations. A June 2017 article on *Yahoo! Finance* shows recent pictures of each of the 32 female CEOs running Fortune 500 companies. None have clearly gray hair.[xc] Even though gray hair might affect people's perception of you, this does not mean these perceptions are right. Perceptions should be questioned, especially if they limit you from expressing your personal brand and being who you are built to be.

Overweight women are judged more harshly by employers. They're more likely to face discrimination when applying for a job. The BBC found that employers tend to underestimate the abilities of obese people.[xci] They assume they cannot complete difficult tasks or work for long periods of time without getting tired. Research suggests obese people may be perceived as having less leadership potential.[xcii] Weight bias affects white women particularly strongly. According to Business Insider, 64 pounds links to a 9% decrease in wages.[xciii] Again, these perceptions of people are not correct and can be very unfair. Perceptions that lead to discrimination on weight should be surfaced and questioned. The more important action for you is to foster a workplace environment where leaders are aware of their biases, and make a genuine effort to challenge and eradicate these biases.

A woman's makeup preference may impact her hiring decision. In one study, people were shown photos of the same women wearing no makeup, wearing some makeup and wearing a lot of makeup. In general, research

172

participants preferred the pictures of women in some makeup. According to Dr. Tara Well, a psychology professor at Barnard College of Columbia University, people may think that wearing makeup is linked to self-care and consideration for other unrelated things, like her team and projects; no makeup signaled self-neglect.[xciv] In one survey, 49% of employers said a woman's makeup would be a factor in their hiring decision if the woman were applying for a public-facing role with the company. More than two-thirds of employers in the same survey said they would be less likely to hire a female job applicant who did not wear makeup to an interview.[xcv] This information is not meant to recommend wearing make-up, or the opposite; it simply points out that there are some things that we are in control of and others that we are not, and that these could impact people's perception of us and how we build our personal brands. This does not mean these perceptions are accurate or good. If you choose to confront them, you must continue to nurture an environment where women do not need to conform or change their preferred behavior throughout their careers.

The first step to changing a culture driven by the male perspective is to be aware of these biases, so you can catch yourself and others in the act.

Your digital appearance will influence your marketability as well. There is tremendous value in re-evaluating how you market yourself on your resume and the internet. What will your employer find once they type your name into Google? What if they stumble upon your Facebook, Twitter or Instagram account? On the flipside, what if your interviewer reads your resume and nothing surprises them or stands out? What if there is nothing on your resume that gives your recruiter that sound-bite or hook to justify an interview with your hiring manager?

If you look for "what to think about before interviewing" on websites like *Forbes* and *Business Insider*, you will find suggestions like:
1. What do you know about the company and the position?
2. Have you invested enough time, connections and effort into understanding whether this is a fit?
3. What is the one thing that draws you to this position?
4. How can you harness your skills to adapt to or enhance this role?

These questions are great, but we can do better. The questions that help us prepare for our interviews set the tone at the top for how marketable we appear. For example, if we are asking ourselves, "what do I know about the company?" we produce information that already exists. If we are asking ourselves, "how well do my skills fit this position?" we consider only the skills we already have and draw straight lines to the skills that are currently required for the role.

Your *true* marketability rests in what you bring that is new. You are more than just a new face – you have a different background, with new ideas, new strategies for solving problems, new learnings to drive results and so on. Perhaps this is what makes you unique to your interviewer, and what becomes your *hook*. Ask yourself, "How can I do this differently?" or "What new ideas can I bring?" This raises the bar for you, as well as those interviewing you who believe they have a sound understanding of the job. This strategy might become the pre-sell to being offered a higher role or a quicker promotion.

In my experience interviewing candidates for roles in the companies I have worked for, I have found value in a direct marketability question. Everyone who has interviewed with me will recall my asking them, "Pretend that in every situation you'll be in, the people around you will question why you are in the room. What is that one marketable thing about you? What is the sentence that follows your introduction?"

Your answer needs to be excellent, and here's why. It is important to remember that your interviewer/hiring manager/company will always assume that the person you portray in your interview is "as good as it gets," but with potential to grow. When I interview candidates, I assume this person is at the pinnacle of their marketability. Granted, it is difficult to ace every nanosecond of an interview, but if you fall short, you are unlikely to be offered the benefit of the doubt, especially if other promising candidates are sitting in the waiting room.

Beyond your sense of dress, internet presence and line of questioning, I encourage you to show how intellectually curious you can be, because it shows your potential for performing and enacting change as you brand yourself as a future CEO. We assume that our experience in an interview will be representative of our experience at the company; oftentimes, it is not. If you are able to speak with someone who has extensive exposure to the company prior to your interview, you could mirror them. By saying words and phrases used at the company, you mirror your interviewer and potentially your interviewer's manager, since one of your interviewer's hiring goals is to impress their boss. This kind of mirroring signals to your interviewer that your onboarding process will require minimal effort. These tactics, coupled with a unique brand, will help you get the job you are interviewing for on your path to CEO.

Leveling Up

There is no perfect formula for leveling up, but your brand plays a significant role. This is because for a successful

175

internal promotion, multiple stakeholders have to successfully sell you *up*. I have witnessed conversations where promotions have been approved across companies and industries, and these conversations have revealed a trend:

1. **Your best chance to get promoted is to impress your manager** and directly or indirectly convince them to escalate the decision. This is a lengthier process at larger companies because of added competition, as well as a stringent vetting and succession-planning process. The delay can also be attributed to internal politics. For instance, part of a manager's rationale for promoting an employee will involve justifying that the employees left behind do not deserve to level up. To impress your manager and their superiors, take another page out of a brand marketer's handbook – people dislike to be sold on something, but they love to buy or be in control of a situation. They are more likely to buy when they learn how well your product or services will help them, or what is in it for them. This strategy is also an avenue to seek recognition for your expertise while remaining humble. If you are able to showcase your knowledge while readily admitting where you would need expert opinion, you are faking-it-'til-you-make-it in a more honest way. This way, you impress your manager with your current performance and give them a reason to buy into your immense future potential.

2. **You need one performance conquest and two or three minor wins**. Your conquest would need to be at a scale that garners the attention of your manager's manager and potentially your manager's manager's manager. Your minor wins are your backup dancers, and the proof that your conquest was not a stroke of luck.

3. **You are marketed as someone with more maturity.** Similar to a performance conquest, you should aim to cradle one noteworthy moment that exemplifies your emotional maturity and positive personality traits. In a 2011 Career Builder survey of more than 2,600 hiring managers and HR professionals, 71% said they valued emotional intelligence over IQ, and 75% said they are more likely to promote an employee with high emotional intelligence and a comparatively lower IQ than an employee with a high IQ and low emotional intelligence.[xcvi]

4. **You are not viewed as a flight risk.** Promotions are one of the most significant investments that your company can make in you. You are at a disadvantage if you are recognized as someone who may exit in the near future, or is unlikely to invest in succession planning for yourself and others after your promotion.

5. **"CYA"** – This is a common abbreviation used in the workplace, and stands for "cover your a**." If all else does not result in getting a promotion, your education, employer history and years of experience can be used as an indicator of your future performance. The next chapter will help you charter your long-game path to CEO; one decision you will need to make is to what extent your education versus your years of experience have weight in your personal brand.

When You Get Fired or When You Quit

To build your brand in situations like these, you must position yourself well. Your brand and marketability are important both to the institution you are leaving and to your prospective employer. You should aim to:

1) Maintain or strengthen the compelling nature of the sound-bite or sentence after your name

2) Defend your unique identifier against the inevitability of a stained reputation

When this situation happens:
Anchor your feet firmly on the ground.
- Tolerate discomfort – define pain and practice self-discipline even when it is uncomfortable.
- Live strong values – be courageous, even when your choices are not popular.
- Learn from mistakes – accept responsibility and choose to move forward in a constructive and timely manner.
- Practice perseverance – the most valuable wins are worth waiting for.

Position your head is in the right space.
- Define success – personal success should not be relative to the success of others, unless you have actively invested in trumpeting someone else.
- Maintain healthy boundaries – understand and modify what might be unhealthy, say "no" when you need to and dedicate time to being alone.
- Expend energy intelligently – understand your resource constraints and devote effort to productive causes.
- Calculate risks – deliberately incorporate logic and reasoning into decision-making processes, especially those outside your comfort zone.

Feel the wind in your hair.
- Make peace with the past – reflect on the past to learn from it, not dwell on regrets or grudges.
- Practice gratitude – count blessings rather than burdens, and let your behavior show it.

- Retain personal strength and practice optimism – deflect interactions with negative people and fight the urge to play the blame game.
- Embrace failure and challenges – it is an opportunity to grow wiser and more confident.

My favorite lesson, when it comes to prioritizing marketability in the face of adversity, is to *focus on the things you can control*. While it is important to keep an eye on social media directed at you, it is not necessarily a tool you can fully control.

Rather than wasting energy worrying about *whether* a storm will come, the most marketable people will prepare their brand for the inevitable bad day. They realize that the status of their brand is in their control. As Eleanor Roosevelt said, "no one can make you feel inferior without your consent."

Beyond the Desk Job

The pedestal that you have built for your brand is at risk of collapse if it is not supported by entities beyond your place of employment. With our full-time jobs consuming most of our lives – we spend at least 40% of our awake hours working – it is difficult to commit to almost anything else to further our careers. However, CEOs still devote time, money and energy to personal brand building. They understand that these support structures eventually support their brand, *sans* day job.

The 80/20 rule applies here. Also called the Pareto principle, the rule as applied in business suggests that if you have ten items, two of those items will turn out to be worth more than the other eight items put together. Similarly, the most valuable approaches to building your brand beyond your workplace are:

(1) Being an influential mentor (a topic I covered in the previous chapter).
(2) Building a brand in your community, as an expert on one topic, or a champion of one cause.

To build your brand in your community, create a network of like-minded people in your field and work on connecting deeply. Anyone with genuine expertise is always drawn to other experts, and in their company, you can open up a whole world of new possibilities. Create opportunities where you can be the one in front of a crowd. Find places to talk about your expertise, like clubs, association meetings, conference workshops. The more you speak, the more you will improve, and the more doors will open for you. People do business with people they know, like and trust. The best way for them to remember you is to be seen physically in their space. *Networking* may not always have a positive connotation, but gatherings where the focus is on personal relationships can go far in strengthening your brand outside of work. The success of your brand depends on how well people know about what you offer.

You know you are successful at doing this if your community and your inner circle want to see you win. Your circle should clap the loudest when you have good news. If they do not, find a different cause or a more supportive circle.

Talented women are yet to invest enough time and resources in their brand and marketability. Your brand and marketability are a function of your personality traits. I have witnessed top lawyers, innovators, communicators and even marketers prioritize menial emails over building their brand statement and brand story. We often put our short-term work first, not realizing that a strong personal brand could offer major advantages to how our short-term work is completed.

A study conducted by the Korn Ferry Institute demonstrated that the top six skills that women in senior leadership roles need to develop are (in ascending order): managing ambiguity, displaying courage, directing work, building effective teams, developing talent and⋯. *engaging and inspiring*. How do you engage and inspire? You tell stories.

My main takeaways from about marketability are:

1. Being different can create connections and a sense of belonging.
2. The success of your brand and your ability to market yourself as the face of your community and an influential mentor rests on your core interests, talents, passions and values.
3. Differences can motivate you by strengthening who you are, exposing your opportunities for development and reminding you that you are not the only star in the sky.
4. The more intentional you are with your goals, the closer you will get to articulating the goals that resonate most with you, and the more likely you are to leave a legacy.

Mark Twain said, "It's not the size of the dog in the fight, it's the size of the fight in the dog." Building your unique brand and marketing yourself is a tactic that will take you the extra mile in your journey to CEO. Your unique brand is the cherry on top.

Chapter 10
Your Path(s) Forward

You haven't come this far just to come this far.

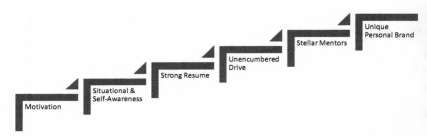

Your path from here to the CEO role will be unique, and it will be shaped by three key questions.

Question 1: How much will I rely on my education versus my experience?

What makes a future CEO great? There have been successful CEOs with vastly different backgrounds and personalities: Warren Buffett, Jack Welch, Indra Nooyi and Steve Jobs, to name just a few. These CEOs are "successful" because of the results they produce and the brands they have built. Their companies have created new products, penetrated new markets, and provided substantial returns to investors and other stakeholders. It is easy to define a CEO as a great leader after his or her company has become successful; what is much more difficult is identifying a great candidate for CEO before that.

Do your indicators of success more heavily skew towards your education or towards your experience? Unless you are a founder of a company, both education and experience are important. You will likely need to balance the two factors in your path to the top. The question is, which one should define you more?

Education > Experience

This is essentially the circumstance where the perception of your education creates an impact that is equal to or greater than the value of the results you have delivered while working. Your audience is your direct manager in your early career, and the Board of Directors when you are gunning for the CEO role. For example, when your resume is flaunted in front of a Board of Directors who are in the process of picking a CEO, your main selling points are what you studied, where you went to school and the number of degrees you have, over the results you delivered over your career.

If this is the case, a bachelor's degree is a minimum requirement, and you will certainly need more than a participation medal.

What you studied could make a difference. Today, Boards favor degrees in business-related subjects when choosing a CEO. Just over half of Fortune 100 CEOs have a degree in business, economics or accounting, while 27% studied engineering or science and 14% studied law. In the future, this could change. Here are some strong areas of study that will help you build the skills you need to be a successful CEO:

- **Business.** Studying business management will teach you about the big picture managements of a business, not just the day-to-day grind.
- **Economics.** Studying economics gives you an understanding of the world we live in, from what determines the price of goods and services to macro-factors that influence standards of living.
- **Accounting and Finance.** Similar to studying business, pursuing a degree in accounting and finance will give you a great base level of knowledge and understanding of how a business works. The real difference is that accounting and finance degrees will have a heavier focus on numbers.
- **Engineering or Science.** While half of Fortune 100 CEOs studied business, economics, or accounting, 27% of the CEOs on the list studied engineering or the sciences (the largest percentage of any one subject). Transferrable skills from the sciences – like logic-based decision making and analytical capabilities – are applicable in the business world.
- **Liberal Arts.** A liberal arts degree can help you gain knowledge in a number of different areas, to adapt to changing business climates and needs of the stakeholders that govern companies – the shareholders, Board of Directors and employees.

Does where you went to school make a difference? Of Fortune 500 CEOs, 9.2% attended Ivy League universities, 3.6% did not attend university and the rest attended public and private universities at equal rates.[xcvii]

The exclusivity of top tier schools represent your ability to outperform the majority, and possibly those in the boardroom. Additionally, it does not hurt if one of the

Directors hiring a CEO shares your alma mater, especially if this Director is proud of where they went to school. Elite schools also have more resources to equip their students with knowledge, connections and starter jobs in order to achieve their life goals. These students may not have to dedicate as much time to researching career options or networking with prospective employers.

Having an advanced degree could make a difference. Today, over a third of Fortune 500 CEOs have MBAs. Harvard Law School found that in a sample of over 14,000 CEOs, MBAs were the most prevalent advanced degrees. The MBA outranked Law Schools, Top 20 Law Schools, other master's degrees and degrees from Top 20 undergraduate schools. The study also compared the education of a CEO to company performance and found that firms with CEOs holding an MBA performed better than those with CEOs holding a law degree.

Most notably, an *elite* MBA will not significantly increase your chances of becoming a CEO over an MBA from non-elite schools. This is consistent with the Fortune 500 CEOs as well. Only 25% of the women and 16% of the men from the Fortune 500 hold an MBA from a top-ten school.[xcviii] The CEO Genome Project, a data set of more than 17,000 C-suite executive assessments over 10 years has identified "CEO sprinters" – those who reached the CEO role faster than the average of 24 years from their first job. One-quarter of sprinters had elite MBAs – but three-quarters did not.

Experience > Education
Here, you are positioning yourself to prove that your "I Can" is more than your IQ. The Board of Directors will be

looking for the basics – knowledge of corporate finance, specific personality traits – and will be influenced by how you have marketed yourself.

Today, Boards are looking for veterans at the CEO role. More corporations have exhibited a preference for hiring former CEOs, as part of their CEO succession planning. Between 2007 and 2009, almost 20% of the newly appointed CEOs had CEO experience at another corporation. This is compared to fewer than 5% between 1995 and 2002. This dramatic increase may be driven by an unwillingness, on the Board's part, to take the risk of hiring individuals with no previous job–specific experience. Hiring organizations may assume that CEO job–specific experience offers both a valid track record and expertise around what it takes to operate as a CEO.[xcix]

If you are aiming for career successes that carry you to the CEO position, you will need to aim high, and check the following experiences off the list:

You should have Board experience: One of the positions you should aim to check off your list is membership on a Board. A Board of Directors needs to agree that you have what it takes, and they are more likely to feel this way if you have Board experience and existing understanding of company governance.

Over 45% of CEOs served as non–executive directors on public company boards before being named CEO of the Fortune 500 companies they lead today.[c] You could also view Board experience as a form of professional development – you will learn from other executives from different industries, get exposure to different governance practices and understand the CEO role through the eyes of the Board. The Board views it as a rite of passage that gives future CEOs an understanding of the bigger picture. Keep an eye out for opportunities like this at smaller companies, start-ups and non-profits in your early and mid-career.

You should have Merger & Acquisition (M&A) experience: The technical skills garnered from an understanding of financial modeling and P&L management will always be a plus in the business world. M&A experience, in particular, will help you apply these skills to the nuanced business world, where soft-skills could be as important. This experience exercises the ability to cultivate business relationships and make decisions with conviction. Doing this well is also an indication of strong change management (the approach to prepare, support and help individuals, teams, and organizations in making organizational change) and long-term strategic planning. In one survey, 91% of those who were surveyed said that the most successful employees are the ones who can adapt to the changing workplace.[ci] The highly adaptable CEOs that the researchers analyzed spent up to half of their time strategizing for the future rather than reacting to short-term changes.[cii] In other words, they are researching potential obstacles by tapping into their business channels rather than waiting for problems to arise. Jump on an M&A project at the company you work in, or learn from a friend or colleague who does this for a living. For a deeper understanding, apply for M&A positions within or outside your place of work.

You should have Crisis Management experience: More than 30% of CEO "sprinters" identified by the CEO Genome project led their teams through a big mess they inherited, such as an unsuccessful product, underachieving business division, or even bankruptcy. In most cases, they fixed it. Successful leaders, in the wake of a crisis, recognize that they have been presented with an opportunity to demonstrate positive governance and emotional maturity. In situations where perception matters more than reality, they may also seize the moment to under-promise and over-deliver – a strategy that could double their credibility. If you are able to manage your ego through the valleys and peaks of a major business crisis, the Board of Directors will take notice. Try not to be afraid of inheriting a mess. Take bold actions to fix problems.

Ideally, you should have experience operating at an executive level. Those that are operating at an executive level already will find themselves at the top of the pile for the CEO role. This is because they already have the resume, the situational leadership and self-awareness, unencumbered drive and possibly a unique brand to be a successful CEO. In March 2019, the Fortune 500 got word of an additional female CEO in the pipeline, when Gap Inc. announced that it is spinning off its Old Navy brand into its own publicly-traded company in 2020. Her name is Sonia Syngal, and she has been president and CEO of Old Navy since 2016. Sonia took the insider track – she first joined parent Gap Inc. in 2004 as the vice president of sourcing strategy; then she served as senior vice president of Old Navy's international business and executive vice president for Gap's global supply chain and product operations. Her performance in these positions proved she was undoubtedly operating at an executive level, and could excel in the CEO role.

Many senior leaders I have worked with assume that you must be a CFO to become a CEO, but this is not true. While a foundation in finance is an important building block for a career, only *5%* of Fortune 500 CEOs were promoted directly from CFO. Companies value the skills of a strong operator more – over half were appointed from the role of COO or President. A CEO I worked for theorized that, in a larger operating company, this pipeline to CEO is more likely to come from the Chief Financial Officer (CFO) or Chief Operating Officer (COO). In a younger or rapidly growing company, you wield more power as a manager of a product, like a Chief Marketing Officer (CMO), Chief Technology Officer (CTO), Chief Sales Officer or Chief Strategy Officer. This is possibly because a company's Board of Directors aims to match the company's future direction with the forte of the CEO they pick. Typically, a growing company will benefit from strong marketing, advanced technology, more robust sales and smart strategy, over a focus on only financial performance and operations. I encourage you to test this theory – from which executive role will you be promoted to CEO from?

What experience can I get in my early career to acquaint myself with the rigors of being CEO?
I was Chief of Staff (COS) to a CEO early in my career. I was accountable for making life easier for the CEO I reported up to, by saving him time to focus on bigger picture decisions. I was also involved in cross-functional projects across the company. During my time in the role, I met with the CEO every day he was in the office. Sometimes, I was a fly on the wall in meetings; other times, I was an active participant. Every so often, I would have one-on-one leadership and learning lessons with him,

189

where he handed over pebbles of wisdom that I would have had to wait 20 years to learn on my own.

If you are in the early stage of your career, I recommend the role as a path to CEO if you understand the following expectations:

1) As Chief of Staff (COS), you should be aiming to be a future CEO. The COS role is a stepping stone to roles that will more effectively cultivate your financial and interpersonal skills as well as your personal brand.

2) It is not an easy role. You are probably working for one of the most expensive and often the most driven people. You understand your primary purpose – to calculate the value of the CEO's time, preserve that value and attempt to enhance it. You must balance this with valuing your own time. This means:

   Little Work-Life Balance and Flexibility: This is not a 9 to 5 job and you will be expected to respond to emails, texts and calls after hours. You will work on most weekends to preserve the value of your CEO's time.

   Exceptional Communication Skills & Emotional Intelligence: You must adjust your communication strategy to your audience e.g. a BLUF (Bottom Line Up Front) when with the CEO, but a different strategy when you converse with entry-level team members. You should also understand how to build trust, always appear as a team player and use different methods of communication to navigate through different situations, like an effective way to convey urgency without causing panic.

   Thick Skin: You must manage people through difficult times, deliver bad news, fix problems and do many things the CEO would prefer not to do. After all, your job is to save his time and mental energy.

Despite the demands of the role, my Chief of Staff experience was extremely rewarding. I garnered the motivation to be CEO, received on-the-job training for what is needed to go the extra mile to succeed as a CEO, and was then promoted into a job that challenged me to fine-tune my financial and inter-personal skills.

How do I know if the COS role is wrong for me?

This decision will rest on how willing your CEO is to create future CEOs. Good CEOs will expect a COS to lead, not just support. They will look to hire someone they can learn from, because the purpose of hiring should be to build a pipeline of future leaders. If a CEO hires someone into this right-hand role, and expects this employee to only *support*, and not *lead*, it raises multiple red flags:

- **The CEO might not understand the importance of or see her role in succession planning.** Succession planning for the CEO role is applicable to executive positions *and* those at the bottom of the corporate pyramid. The COS role is an ideal training ground for creating future CEOs, and a candidate should be picked using that lens.
- **The CEO might not fully understand the value of time.** The COS is potentially the single best return on investment (ROI) a CEO could make in the workplace – the COS on a mid-level salary will save the time of the most expensive person in the company on a daily basis. The ROI is even higher if someone in the COS role develops the potential to be a feeder role to the executive level.
- **The CEO might not understand her role in setting the tone at the top for company culture.** Think about the message this would send to the company. A CEO who sets the expectation that there is a ceiling for

191

leadership and responsibilities, for the role that they have 100% control over (like the COS role), is not encouraging a culture of development and growth.

If you choose the Chief of Staff route, pick your CEO wisely. Beyond that, it is up to you to determine how much you want your brand to be weighted on your education versus your experience.

Question 2: Do I prefer to follow the proven path or am I willing to take risks with my career?

Chapter 9 outlines what it may take to get promoted. Your path to CEO will require multiple promotions through two different paths. You get to pick which one you would like to follow more closely.

Option 1: The Proven Path
The inside track and a show of decades of loyalty have been the most prominent influencers for the appointment of these women to Fortune 500 CEO positions.

The youngest woman in the group in 2018, Heather Bresch, was age 45 when she was appointed CEO. Her story at Mylan champions the insider track – in her case, for 20 years. This is a popular track among the group of female CEOs. Over 20% of them now run the companies they joined right after their education, and 70% spent more than ten years before being promoted to CEO (compared to 48% of male CEOs).[ciii]

Note that none of these opportunities were as *glamorous* as the ones they have now. Heather Bresch began her career as a clerk in a factory owned by Mylan; Mary Barra, the CEO of General Motors, started out with the company as a college co-op student. Other women on the list delayed their jump onto the business track. Only three had a job at a banking or consulting firm right after college, and made lateral moves into the positions they are in today.

Loyalty also proves to be fruitful with other groups of CEOs. Take the Fortune 100: *51%* of this group of CEOs have spent 20 years or more working for the companies they now head. Outside the U.S., loyalty is even more valued, with *75%* of non-U.S. CEOs spending 35 years or more at the same company.[civ]

Here are some more success stories that make it compelling to choose the proven path:

- *Number of companies:* Not one CEO at America's 100 biggest companies has been with more than five companies in the span of their careers: *31%* have been with only one other company, 12% with two other companies and *13%* with three or more.
- *Age of joining:* 15% joined their companies directly after graduating from college. An additional *35%* started their professional careers at the company they currently lead.
- *Level of investment:* Five CEOs are the founders of their company.
- *Loyalty over pride:* Four began their careers with the companies they are now in charge of, then left and rejoined later.

However, the "inside track" strategy and loyalty are wasted if your workplace is not a fit for you. Do not commit decades to the inside track at the *first* company you join. I believe it is important to actively evaluate every company you are at, to determine whether you could and should move up the ranks to CEO there. Consider these factors when you conduct your evaluation (and remember that in every interview, you should evaluate the company as much as they evaluate you).

Where are *YOU* in this role?

Sure, part of the job is being able to deliver what the cookie-cutter job description asked of you. It is just as important to identify whether your current role offers growth opportunities within the role or move into another role that offers more. Look past the laundry list of the skills and qualifications your company wants you to have and determine if your current place of work not only has a role that fits your skills but invests in your path to CEO.

If not, consider moving roles within the company, and use the pointers in *Chapter 9* to position yourself well in internal and external interviews.

Where are *YOU* in this company?

You might be ready to shine and move up, but your company might not be positioned to encourage this or make a promotion happen for you. Ask yourself – does my place of work:

- Have the *organizational structure* to promote to CEO, or is there a lack of order where promotional decisions are based on workplace politics?
- Have the *resources* to support my accelerated development, like funding for training or leadership that I can learn from?
- Have the *Human Resource practices* to ensure that I work in a meritocracy, am protected from unfair treatment and am always evaluated fairly?
- Have the right *culture* for my succession planning? Or do they have little affinity for promoting from within?

194

And finally, ask yourself, "Could I see myself running *this* company?" If the answer is no, and the company you are at still has some of the structure, resources, practices and culture for growth, it might be a great stepping stone but not where you want to land eventually. Before you jump to the decision that you should start looking for job opportunities, however, question *why* you do not see yourself as the CEO of the company, and evaluate whether you could change this for the better in your current and future roles.

<u>Option 2: Making Bold Career Moves Off the Beaten Path</u>
The CEO Genome Project, a study referenced in the previous section, identified "CEO sprinters" – those who became CEO role faster than the average of 24 years from their first job. The study showed that "sprinters" had one thing in common – 97% of them took at least one "catapult" experience, and almost 50% of them had two or more.[cv]
A "catapult" experience is a bold career move that enables you to leapfrog your way up. These experiences may not be easy to navigate at first, but as the old saying goes, storms make a tree's roots deeper. These opportunities rarely fall into your lap – you may need to, as the CEO Genome sprinters stated, "make your own luck." Make a habit of replying "yes" to bold opportunities – ready or not. If you are prepared to travel off the beaten path, you must learn how to (1) potentially embrace unexpected bold moves when they present themselves as opportunities, (2) thrive in uncertain circumstances and (3) manage the risks associated with these moves.

What bold career moves can I make?

- *You could start over* – a new job, a new city, a new industry. When I moved to work for AAA NCNU, I had been to California only once before and was 10,000 miles away from family and across the country from my dearest friends. But the position was the right choice – I received two promotions in three years, and was catapulted to a role where I was running a $2.4 billion business for the company at the age of 26.
- *You could pursue your aspirational goals despite external pressures.* One of my mentors, Laura Furstenthal, did this. She wanted to take business classes but was living in the Bay Area on a $13k stipend/year with her husband and couldn't afford to pay for them herself. So she looked for other programs and despite the pressures of graduate school, attended McKinsey's Insight program, and launched into a new career.
- *You could start something new.* One of my closest friends from college, Annie Garofalo, took a sabbatical from the consulting company she was working for to start a company called MyMerkata to combine ethical fashion with immersive visual storytelling to bring customers closer to their purchases. She moved to Guatemala to launch it.

How can I manage the risks associated with bold career moves?

1. *What am I committing to?* Bold career moves are never completely painless. But while sink-or-swim situations are energizing, a handy safety net can be an exit clause – a way to reverse or abandon a bold move if it does not materialize as hoped. Your best exit clause will be different in every situation.

2. *Can I endure the risk?* Imagine yourself in the worst possible situation, as a result of your bold move. Have you misplaced all of your resources? Have you lost what is most dear to you? Will you not be able to recover in your lifetime? If the risk is beyond your threshold of tolerance, you may want to shape it to be less committal, or create a contingency plan.

3. *What is the contingency plan?* Don't simply let things take their course and hope for the best. Manage that risk by evaluating the opportunity, your situation and what you can do if things don't work out. When you have high aspirations, caution may be more risky than taking the plunge.

Question 3: When do I want to be CEO?

Despite today's CEOs falling into an "ideal" CEO age range, discussed in *Chapter 1*, you should not hold yourself accountable to any age range. Consider the start-up industry, where the average age of Silicon Valley entrepreneurs who make a successful exit (i.e. sell their company for a bucket-load of money or take it public) is 47 years.[cvi] The world's youngest entrepreneur, Nick D'Aloisio, was only 15 when he received funding for his app Summly, which was later acquired by Yahoo for $38 million.
You could be the exception.

What matters is how you are spending your time.
CEOs have told me that every minute matters in their role, and they understand the value of every minute that has

passed. This switch in mindset, from years to minutes, is an important one to develop early on your path to CEO.

How productive are you with your time? Another way of asking this question is, "How efficiently are you able to complete important tasks?" Efficiency is relative to whether you were able to complete a job at the same or better quality, while expending fewer resources like time and money. Very productive people do not touch something more than once. When they start something, they finish it. This is a common practice among future CEOs, who are always pressed for time.

These are some of the main factors that impact productivity:

Having a purpose. Productive individuals set goals with clear, defined purposes. They dedicate mental energy to crafting their purpose statement and refer back to it regularly. They use purpose statements to weed out responsibilities that do not align with their long-term goals. They have learned how to say no to other people and to themselves. They break down their long-term goals into multiple short-term goals.

Being disciplined. Productive people are usually decisive and disciplined. They focus on one thing at a time. Research has proven time and time again that multitasking risks the loss of your productivity; according to the American Psychology Association, this loss can exceed 40%.[cvii]

Having a productive work time and environment. Productive people take note of productivity peaks. I am most productive in the morning after eight hours of sleep, while sitting upright, surrounded by only a few people in a room with natural sunlight, with a deadline in front of me. There are also a number of techniques to try – the Pomodoro technique encourages you to break your day into half-hour segments. Or, perhaps the Instagram CEO's five-minute trick: when you struggle to start something, tell yourself you are going to do it for five minutes, and, chances are, you will continue straight through until it is complete. How you spend your time will dictate when you become a CEO. Time must be spent and cannot be stopped. As your most valuable resource, time could be your secret weapon for becoming a young CEO, if it is used wisely.

Avoid time sinks on your journey to CEO. Have you ever heard or maybe even experienced first-hand that a microwave minute goes by much slower than an internet minute? Remember that the *value* of your time is under your control. You also control where to invest it and, if invested in your career, you should:

- Preserve this value by avoiding low-value activities (ineffective meetings, too many emails and any conference).
- Incrementally enhance current and future value by adjusting your purpose, support systems and environment to your productive advantage.
- Transform your current and future value by identifying the right people to surround you.

Based on the Money Value of Time theory, the value of your time is possibly highest in your early- and mid-career. The opportunity cost is at an all-time high if this time is squandered.

Avoid meetings without decisions – Meetings are notorious for killing time. They start late, are poorly run and often end without any material accomplishment. Mark Cuban once said, "Never take a meeting unless someone is writing you a check." I worked for a CEO who began every meeting expecting a one-line purpose. For example, "The purpose of this meeting is to inform/discuss/gain approval for…" If the purpose did not warrant his time, he would first politely ask, "Do I need to be here?" and then, more likely than not, would excuse himself respectfully and leave. Better yet, evaluate your calendar at the start of every week – if the purpose of the meeting is not embedded in the invite, or the meeting is unnecessarily long, politely decline.

Watch for the email culture – A poll of over 100 CEOs revealed that too much email is the number one killer of their productivity. When I was Chief of Staff, I conducted an analysis of the real cost of an email. Although they are free to send, they are expensive to read. A study by the University of California-Irvine estimates that it takes upwards of 20 minutes to regain momentum following an interruption.[cviii] Assuming a minimum of 10 minutes for reading the email, I estimated the cost of each company-wide email exceeded $100,000. Some companies send one out every day. This number will be different for your place of work, but I guarantee that the cost will be greater than you expect. In fact, the mere expectation that emails must be flowing in also consumes other moments of real productivity – we are tempted to spend our free moments on email productivity. My advice to you is to set the tone at the top to send fewer emails and check your inbox in a disciplined way. Initially, your team members and colleagues will think you are being unproductive, but in the long term you will be driving the right behavior.

Rethink conferences – There is a reason that most CEOs do not commit too much time to conferences: they cost money and time and produce little economic value. Every time you attend a conference without your team, you become an absent manager. It is unlikely that you will share more than 10% of your learnings with your team when you are back from a conference. I advise that you only attend conferences if:

- *The value provided can be measured in some way* – that every minute spent at the event can be quantified into present and future value.
- *The value exceeds your financial investment* – that it offers more quantifiable value than the sum of the cost to attend, the cost of your salary during the time of attendance *and* the opportunity cost of adding value to your company.
- *Over 75% of the value the event offers is transferable* to your team. Conference planners have no incentive to make the value 100% transferrable. But you should think about how to use what you learn to create more value at work. Some conferences stream seminars or offer follow-up crash courses for your team.

Having a support system. Support systems come in the form of processes, technology and/or people. Productive people will create a support system through practices like asking the right people the right questions and keeping track of where they gain and lose time. My rule is that if I have to perform a task more than twice, I will find an easier way to do it. This is one way you can invest time to create more time in the future.

The people you are surrounded by will influence how you manage your time. This factor drastically influences how you value your time. Being surrounded by productive people does not make you a productive person, especially if you do not value your time or have the optimal support system and environment to make you productive. The main ingredient in the recipe to transform your current and future value of your time is the measure of *how other people value your time*. With only 1,440 minutes in each day, an open-door or talk-to-me-whenever policy in a business environment can sap your productivity. We often forget to account for *distraction time* into our day, which ends up being more damaging than the distraction itself. Although you want to be approachable and respectful, it helps to allocate a period of time each week to helping others or being disciplined about who you assist.

While we often cannot control who we are surrounded by in a workplace, we can influence how people value our time. This is because the main reason why people do not value your time is that you do not value your time. Remove yourself from the equation for a second. Identify leaders who do not value their time. For example, they engage in extensive casual conversation, lack the discipline to meet deadlines and are late to meetings. Often, these same leaders have more cancellations and late-shows than others. They also struggle the most to get other people to hit deadlines. Show the people you are surrounded by that:

- You have a plan for the week before it begins.
- You know who you will be spending your time with, and this is intentional because they too value their time.
- You have a purpose for each meeting you attend and each meeting is part of a larger goal.

- You are most productive when you are at your workstation.

Others value your time exactly as you do. You control how you value your time – you know how to calculate it and enhance it. Additionally, someone who values their time encourages and inspires others to value their time as well. This is a key quality of a future CEO.

Conclusion:
Surgite

You have not come this far just to come this far. As the CEO who convinced me that I could be a CEO one day told me, "Surgite!" – Latin for "Push on".

2018 saw a 25% decline in the number of women leading Fortune 500 companies. While 2017 hit an all-time high for number of women in these positions, the number was still only 6.4%. You can change this number, because you and the women around you are built to be CEO.

For me, this journey began on International Women's Day.

On March 8th 2018, the women I work with and my friends who motivate me every day (too many to name, but you know who you are) effervescently celebrated *International Women's Day*. Their inspirational messages and stories reminded me that a good role model is all it takes to change someone's life. John F. Kennedy said, "one person can make a difference, and everyone should try it." I began compiling content that has shaped much of this piece of work. And I began writing, and embodying the advice I wrote down.

For you, the journey started when you said, out loud, that you are built to be CEO. And the journey doesn't conclude until you get there.

RECAP

Motivation in your early career:

Introduction – You Haven't Come This Far Just To Come This Far: The typical CEO in today's world bears a striking physical and behavioral resemblance to a male North American moose. You, on the other hand, might be a unicorn. The physical characteristics of a *future* CEO can be shaped by you.

Chapter 1: Do You Want to be CEO? The CEO position could be for you. One of the primary factors in connecting women to the CEO position, according to studies, is being told that it is possible to be a CEO. By becoming CEO, you could change some disappointing trends – only 6.4% of Fortune 500 companies were run by female CEOs in 2017, which is 15 times fewer women than men.

Chapter 2: Time is Your Most Valuable Player (MVP). Time is a resource far more valuable than money. Women, in many instances, are not equally compensated as men for their time. Using your time effectively in your early career to build your upward trajectory and fulfill your aspirational goals could transform and accelerate your path to CEO.

Understand What You're Getting Into

Chapter 3: The Force Fields in Your Environment. Biochemistry may not be holding women back from being CEO, but Hollywood could be a contributing factor starting from childhood. The industry limits female succession planning through its pervasive stereotypes and shortage of role models.

Chapter 4: The Types and Traits of CEOs. There are a number of key personality traits that future CEOs must develop to accelerate their career, align their personal goals with their professional goals and embody successful traits early on.

Chapter 5: A List of Excuses. I have dedicated this chapter to listing excuses, because I want to ensure they do not obstruct you from becoming a CEO.

Start Your Training Early

Chapter 6: The Resume Builder. There are not too many technical skills required to become CEO, versus personality and leadership skills. What is non-negotiable is a deep understanding of and some experience in corporate finance.

Chapter 7: The Agenda Drivers. In business, you are going to need to know how to convince people about yourself and your ideas. You will need to learn how to establish trust, change the conversation, pay attention to body language, anticipate criticism, be aware of your biases and dispel stereotypes about women.

Chapter 8: The Support Boosters. You do not have to travel alone on your path to the top of the pyramid. Find your mentors, sponsors and supporters early on in your career and pay their support forward to other young women who could benefit from learning from you.

Chapter 9: The Cherry on Top. While men tend to remove junior-level roles from their LinkedIn profiles, women publish 11% fewer skills than men. It is time for women to build unique personal brands and advertise the value they add to their workplace, industry and community.

And finally, *Chapter 10: Your Path(s) Forward.*

END

NOTES

[i] "The Breakthrough Formula: WOMEN CEOs." New Research Shows Women Are Better at Using Soft Skills Crucial for Effective Leadership and Superior Business Performance, Finds Korn Ferry Hay Group – Media & Press, www.kornferry.com /institute/the-breakthrough-formula-women-ceos

[ii] Lublin, Joann S. "Though Outnumbered, Female CEOs Earn More Than Male Chiefs." The Wall Street Journal, Dow Jones & Company, 31 May 2017, www.wsj.com/articles/women-ceos-dont-get-paid-less-than-men-in-big-business-they-make-more-1496223001.

[iii] Bolshaw, Liz. "Is the X Chromosome the X Factor for Business Leadership?" Home, EY, 3 July 2018, www.ey.com/en_gl/growth/growth-barometer-diversity.

[iv] Miller, Claire Cain, et al. "The Top Jobs Where Women Are Outnumbered by Men Named John." The New York Times, The New York Times, 24 Apr. 2018, www.nytimes.com/interactive/2018/04/24/upshot/women-and-men-named-john.html.

[v] Krivkovich, Alexis, et al. "Women in the Workplace 2017." McKinsey & Company, www.mckinsey.com/featured-insights/gender-equality/women-in-the-workplace-2017.

[vi] "The Share of Female CEOs in the Fortune 500 Dropped by 25% in 2018." Fortune, Fortune, fortune.com/2018/05/21/women-fortune-500-2018/.

[vii] Mohr, Tara Sophia. "Why Women Don't Apply for Jobs Unless They're 100% Qualified."Harvard Business Review, 2 Mar. 2018, hbr.org/2014/08/why-women-dont-apply-for-jobs-unless-theyre-100-qualified.

[viii] "The Breakthrough Formula: WOMEN CEOs." New Research Shows Women Are Better at Using Soft Skills Crucial for Effective

Leadership and Superior Business Performance, Finds Korn Ferry Hay Group – Media & Press, www.kornferry.com/institute/the-breakthrough-formula-women-ceos

[ix] Frick, Walter. "Are Most CEOs Too Old to Innovate?" Harvard Business Review, 6 Dec. 2017, hbr.org/2014/11/are-most-ceos-too-old-to-innovate.

[x] Jones, Del. "Does Age Matter When You're CEO?" ABC News, ABC News Network, 11 Sept. 2008, abcnews.go.com/Business/story?id=5568622&page=1.

[xi] Nanji, Ayaz. "The Average Age and Tenure of C-Suite Executives." MarketingProfs, MarketingProfs, 9 Mar. 2017, www.marketingprofs.com/charts/2017/31713/the-average-age-and-tenure-of-c-suite-executives.

[xii] Lee-Woolf, Yoke Har, et al. "The Average Age of CEOs at Startups Is Creeping up, so Is the Average Age of Nobel Prize Winners. Why Age and Wisdom Still Matter." Idealog, 27 Nov. 2014, idealog.co.nz/venture/2014/11/average-startup-founders-age-creeping-so-average-age-nobel-prize-winners-why-age-and-wisdom-still-matter.

[xiii] Frick, Walter. "Are Most CEOs Too Old to Innovate?" Harvard Business Review, 6 Dec. 2017, hbr.org/2014/11/are-most-ceos-too-old-to-innovate.

[xiv] Jones, Del. "Does Age Matter When You're CEO?" ABC News, ABC News Network, 11 Sept. 2008, abcnews.go.com/Business/story?id=5568622&page=1.

[xv] Pradit, and Pornsit. "CEO Age and CEO Gender: Are Female CEOs Older Than Their Male Counterparts?" By John Cigno :: SSRN, 4 Jan. 2017, papers.ssrn.com/sol3/papers.cfm?abstract_id=2891911.

[xvii] "More People Enroll in College Even with Rising Price Tag, Report Finds." Esports Quickly Expanding in Colleges, Inside Higher Ed, www.insidehighered.com/news/2016/09/22/more-people-enroll-college-even-rising-price-tag-report-finds.

[xviii] Björnberg, Åsa, and Claudio Feser. "CEO Succession Starts with Developing Your Leaders."McKinsey & Company, www.mckinsey.com/featured-insights/leadership/ceo-succession-starts-with-developing-your-leaders.

[xix] Fletcher, Thandi. "Using Money to Buy Time Linked to Increased Happiness." UBC News, 21 Nov. 2017, news.ubc.ca/2017/07/24/using-money-to-buy-time-linked-to-increased-happiness/.

[xx] Karlsson, Ken FavaroPer-Ola, and Gary L. Neilson. "The Lives and Times of the CEO." Strategy+Business, 30 May 2014, www.strategy-business.com/feature/00254?gko=88288.

[xxi] Murphy, Heather. "Picture a Leader. Is She a Woman?" The New York Times, The New York Times, 16 Mar. 2018, www.nytimes.com/2018/03/16/health/women-leadership-workplace.html.

[xxii] "Bechdel Test." Wikipedia, Wikimedia Foundation, 16 June 2018, en.wikipedia.org/wiki/Bechdel_test.

[xxiii] Saxena, Jaya. "Women Had a Third of Speaking Roles in Movies in the Past Ten Years."ELLE, ELLE, 8 Oct. 2017, www.elle.com/culture/movies-tv/news/a47090/women-underrepresented-in-film-study-usc/.

[xxiv] Petreikis, John. "Research." Center for the Study of Women in Television and Film, Center for the Study of Women in Television and Film, 16 June 2016, womenintvfilm.sdsu.edu/research/.

[xxv] Petreikis, John. "Research." Center for the Study of Women in Television and Film, Center for the Study of Women in Television and Film, 16 June 2016, womenintvfilm.sdsu.edu/research/.

[xxvi] Petreikis, John. "Research." Center for the Study of Women in Television and Film, Center for the Study of Women in Television and Film, 16 June 2016, womenintvfilm.sdsu.edu/research/.

[xxvii] Carpentier, Megan. "Why, in 2016, Are Women Still (Mostly) Silent Film Stars?" The Guardian, Guardian News and Media, 12 Apr. 2016, www.theguardian.com/film/2016/apr/12/women-film-speaking-roles-2016-study-hollywood.

[xxviii] McLean, Craig. "Is Disney Sexist? - BBC Three." BBC, BBC, 11 Dec. 2017, www.bbc.co.uk/bbcthree/article/24e20f4c-5f17-45fa-9179-f8a9fdccbe9a.

[xxix] McLean, Craig. "Is Disney Sexist? - BBC Three." BBC, BBC, 11 Dec. 2017, www.bbc.co.uk/bbcthree/article/24e20f4c-5f17-45fa-9179-f8a9fdccbe9a.

[xxx] Womenandhollywood.com, womenandhollywood.com/resources/statistics/.

[xxxi] Chira, Susan, and Brianna Milord. "'Is There a Man I Can Talk To?': Stories of Sexism in the Workplace." The New York Times, The New York Times, 20 June 2017, www.nytimes.com/2017/06/20/business/women-react-to-sexism-in-the-workplace.html.

[xxxii] Greenfield, Rebecca, and Laura Colby. "Sexual Harassment Helps Explain Why Women Get Paid Less." Los Angeles Times, Los Angeles Times, www.latimes.com/business/la-fi-sex-harassment-women-pay-20180114-story.html.

[xxxiii] Dougherty, Debbie S. "The Omissions That Make So Many Sexual Harassment Policies Ineffective." Harvard Business Review, 7

July 2017, hbr.org/2017/05/the-omissions-that-make-so-many-sexual-harassment-policies-ineffective.

[xxxiv] Silverstein, Melissa. "Statistics." IndieWire, Indiewire, 24 Feb. 2014, www.indiewire.com/2014/02/statistics-240754/.

[xxxv] "Women in Film: Identity and Power." ADD / ADHD – Attention Deficit Disorder, talentdevelop.com/articles/wifip.html.

[xxxvi] Berman, Jillian. "Here's How Long It'll Take To Close The Gender Wage Gap In Each State."The Huffington Post, TheHuffingtonPost.com, 7 Dec. 2017, www.huffingtonpost.com/2015/03/13/gender-wage-gap-close_n_6863314.html.

[xxxvii] "Pay Equity Information." National Committee on Pay Equity NCPE, www.pay-equity.org/info-time.html.

[xxxviii] "The Pay Gap Is Far From the Only Discrimination Women Face." *Time*, Time, time.com/5562441/equal-pay-wage-punishment-gap/?amp=true.

[xxxix] "Women in Film: Identity and Power." ADD / ADHD – Attention Deficit Disorder, talentdevelop.com/articles/wifip.html.

[xl] Burkus, David. "Everyone Likes Flex Time, but We Punish Women Who Use It." Harvard Business Review, 20 Feb. 2017, hbr.org/2017/02/everyone-likes-flex-time-but-we-punish-women-who-use-it.

[xli] Shafrir, Doree. "Tech Companies Prove the Old Boys' Club Is Alive and Well." New York Post, New York Post, 29 Apr. 2017, nypost.com/2017/04/29/tech-companies-prove-the-old-boys-club-is-alive-and-well/.

[xlii] Womenandhollywood.com, womenandhollywood.com/resources/statistics/.

xliii "Women in Film: Identity and Power." ADD / ADHD – Attention Deficit Disorder, talentdevelop.com/articles/wifip.html.

xliv "Myers Briggs Statistics." Statistic Brain, Statistic Brain, 1 Oct. 2017, www.statisticbrain.com/myers-briggs-statistics/.

xlv Kerwin, Patrick L. True Type Tales: Real Stories about the Power of Personality Type in Everyday Life. Patrick L. Kerwin, 2013.
xlvi "The Facets of the Entrepreneur: Identifying Entrepreneurial Potential." Emeraldinsight, www.emeraldinsight.com/doi/abs/10.1108/00251740410515861.

xlvii "The Big Five and Venture Survival: Is There a Linkage?" *Egyptian Journal of Medical Human Genetics*, Elsevier, 30 Oct. 2003, www.sciencedirect.com/science/article/abs/pii/S0883902603000934.

xlviii Elena Lytkina BotelhoKim Rosenkoetter PowellStephen KincaidDina Wang. "4 Things That Set Successful CEOs Apart." Harvard Business Review, 18 July 2017, hbr.org/2017/05/what-sets-successful-ceos-apart.

xlix Orr, Jane Edison StevensonEvelyn. "We Interviewed 57 Female CEOs to Find Out How More Women Can Get to the Top." Harvard Business Review, 8 Nov. 2017, hbr.org/2017/11/we-interviewed-57-female-ceos-to-find-out-how-more-women-can-get-to-the-top.

l "Learning from Mum: Cross-National Evidence Linking Maternal Employment and Adult Children's Outcomes." Work, Employment and Society, journals.sagepub.com/doi/abs/10.1177/0950017018760167.

li Council, Forbes Coaches. "If You Want To Be 'CEO Material,' Develop These 15 Traits." Forbes, Forbes Magazine, 29 Dec. 2017, www.forbes.com/sites/forbescoachescouncil/2017/12/29/if-you-want-to-be-ceo-material-develop-these-15-traits/.

[lii] Council, Forbes Coaches. "If You Want To Be 'CEO Material,' Develop These 15 Traits." Forbes, Forbes Magazine, 29 Dec. 2017, www.forbes.com/sites/forbescoachescouncil/2017/12/29/if-you-want-to-be-ceo-material-develop-these-15-traits/.

[liii] Council, Forbes Coaches. "If You Want To Be 'CEO Material,' Develop These 15 Traits." Forbes, Forbes Magazine, 29 Dec. 2017, www.forbes.com/sites/forbescoachescouncil/2017/12/29/if-you-want-to-be-ceo-material-develop-these-15-traits/.

[liv] Council, Forbes Coaches. "If You Want To Be 'CEO Material,' Develop These 15 Traits." Forbes, Forbes Magazine, 29 Dec. 2017, www.forbes.com/sites/forbescoachescouncil/2017/12/29/if-you-want-to-be-ceo-material-develop-these-15-traits/

[lv] Patten, Eileen. "How American Parents Balance Work and Family Life When Both Work." Pew Research Center, Pew Research Center, 4 Nov. 2015, www.pewresearch.org/fact-tank/2015/11/04/how-american-parents-balance- work-and-family-life-when-both-work/.

[lvi] St-Onge, Astrid JaekelElizabeth. "Why Women Aren't Making It to the Top of Financial Services Firms." Harvard Business Review, 17 Nov. 2016, hbr.org/2016/10/why-women-arent-making-it-to-the-top-of-financial-services-firms.

[lvii] "Ross Perot Quotes." BrainyQuote, Xplore, www.brainyquote.com/quotes/ross_perot_101658.

[lviii] Guillen, Laura. "Is the Confidence Gap Between Men and Women a Myth?" Harvard Business Review, 26 Mar. 2018, hbr.org/2018/03/is-the-confidence-gap-between-men-and-women-a-myth.

[lix] Cole, Samantha. "How To Disarm A Defensive Audience." Fast Company, Fast Company, 30 July 2015, www.fastcompany.com/3040749/how-to-disarm-a-defensive-audience.

lx Cole, Samantha. "How To Disarm A Defensive Audience." Fast Company, Fast Company, 30 July 2015, www.fastcompany.com/3040749/how-to-disarm-a-defensive-audience.

lxi Pelz, James. "5 Phrases and Verbal Tactics to Crush Your Enemies." OnG Blog – OnG.Social The Easiest Way To Cash In On Social Media, alexdev.ong.social/ong-blog/5-phrases-and-verbal-tactics-to-crush-your-enemies.

lxii Pelz, James. "5 Phrases and Verbal Tactics to Crush Your Enemies." OnG Blog – OnG.Social The Easiest Way To Cash In On Social Media, alexdev.ong.social/ong-blog/5-phrases-and-verbal-tactics-to-crush-your-enemies.

lxiii Tabatabaie, Layla. "The Best Ways to Respond to an Insult, According to Steve Jobs."Ladders | Business News & Career Advice, Ladders | Business News & Career Advice, 25 Oct. 2017, www.theladders.com/career-advice/best-ways-respond-insult-according-steve-jobs.

lxiv "Affect Heuristic – Biases & Heuristics | The Decision Lab." The Decision Lab – Behavioral Science, Applied., thedecisionlab.com/bias/affect-heuristic/.

lxv Goudreau, Jenna. "The 10 Worst Stereotypes About Powerful Women." Forbes, Forbes Magazine, 13 May 2012,www.forbes.com/sites/jennagoudreau/2011/10/24/worst-stereotypes-powerful-women-christine-lagarde-hillary-clinton/2/#70f5151e504a.=

lxvi Flynn, Kathryn HeathJill. "How Women Can Show Passion at Work Without Seeming 'Emotional.'" Harvard Business Review, 30 Sept. 2015, hbr.org/2015/09/how-women-can-show-passion-at-work-without-seeming-emotional.

lxvii Carnegie Mellon University. "Researchers Find Everyone Has a Bias Blind Spot – News – Carnegie Mellon University." Culture and Environment, www.cmu.edu/news/stories/archives/2015/june/bias-blind-spot.html.

lxviii Uzzi, Brian. "Research: Men and Women Need Different Kinds of Networks to Succeed." Harvard Business Review, 26 Feb. 2019, hbr.org/2019/02/research-men-and-women-need-different-kinds-of-networks-to-succeed.

lxix Prasad, Ritu. "Seven Ways the World Is Not Designed for Women." *BBC News*, BBC, 28 Mar. 2019, www.bbc.com/news/world-us-canada-47725946?ocid=socialflow_facebook.

lxx Greenbaum, Karen. "Measuring the Positive Impact of Women on Businesses." LinkedIn, 12 June 2018, www.linkedin.com/pulse/measuring-positive-impact-women-businesses-karen-greenbaum/.

lxxi Krivkovich, Alexis, et al. "Women in the Workplace 2017." McKinsey & Company, www.mckinsey.com/featured-insights/gender-equality/women-in-the-workplace-2017.

lxxii Orr, Jane Edison StevensonEvelyn. "We Interviewed 57 Female CEOs to Find Out How More Women Can Get to the Top." Harvard Business Review, 8 Nov. 2017, hbr.org/2017/11/we-interviewed-57-female-ceos-to-find-out-how-more-women-can-get-to-the-top.

lxxiii Nhendryx. "The Bottom Line: Connecting Corporate Performance and Gender Diversity." Catalyst, 12 Apr. 2013, www.catalyst.org/knowledge/bottom-line-connecting-corporate-performance-and-gender-diversity.

lxxiv "The Mix That Matters: Innovation Through Diversity." Https://Www.bcg.com, 26 Apr. 2017, www.bcg.com/en-us/publications/2017/people-organization-leadership-talent-innovation-through-diversity-mix-that-matters.aspx.

lxxv Donald, Professor Dame Athene, and Professor of experimental physics at the University of Cambridge. "67% Of Europeans Don't Believe Women Have the Skills to Be Scientists."The Guardian, Guardian News and Media, 24 Sept. 2015, www.theguardian.com/women-in-leadership/2015/sep/24/67-of-europeans-dont-believe-women-have-the-skills-to-be-scientists.

lxxvii "The Trouble With Bright Girls." Psychology Today, Sussex Publishers, www.psychologytoday.com/us/blog/the-science-success/201101/the-trouble-bright-girls.

lxxviii Korn Ferry, "New Research Shows Women Are Better at Using Soft Skills Crucial for Effective Leadership and Superior Business Performance, Finds Korn Ferry Hay Group." March 4, 2016 http://www.kornferry.com/press/new-research-shows-women-are-better-at-using-soft-skills-crucial-for-effective-leadership/

lxxix Donald, Professor Dame Athene, and Professor of experimental physics at the University of Cambridge. "67% Of Europeans Don't Believe Women Have the Skills to Be Scientists."The Guardian, Guardian News and Media, 24 Sept. 2015, www.theguardian.com/women-in-leadership/2015/sep/24/67-of-europeans-dont-believe-women-have-the-skills-to-be-scientists.

lxxx "Can an Angry Woman Get Ahead?: Status Conferral, Gender, and Expression of Emotion in the Workplace." Gender Action Portal, 1 Jan. 1970, gap.hks.harvard.edu/can-angry-woman-get-ahead-status-conferral-gender-and-expression-emotion-workplace.

lxxxi Korn Ferry, "New Research Shows Women Are Better at Using Soft Skills Crucial for Effective Leadership and Superior Business Performance, Finds Korn Ferry Hay Group." March 4, 2016 http://www.kornferry.com/press/new-research-shows-women-are-better-at-using-soft-skills-crucial-for-effective-leadership/

lxxxii "Why Do Women Outnumber Men in College?" NBER, University of Chicago Press, www.nber.org/digest/jan07/w12139.html.

217

[lxxxiii] Korn Ferry, "New Research Shows Women Are Better at Using Soft Skills Crucial for Effective Leadership and Superior Business Performance, Finds Korn Ferry Hay Group." March 4, 2016 http://www.kornferry.com/press/new-research-shows-women-are-better-at-using-soft-skills-crucial-for-effective-leadership/

[lxxxiv] Krivkovich, Alexis, et al. "Women in the Workplace 2017." McKinsey & Company, www.mckinsey.com/featured-insights/gender-equality/women-in-the-workplace-2017.

[lxxxv] Fessler, Leah. "The Simple, Damning Difference between Women's and Men's Profiles on LinkedIn." *Quartz*, Quartz, 29 Aug. 2017, qz.com/1064803/the-simple-damning-difference-between-women-and-mens-profiles-on-linkedin/.

[lxxxvi] "Enclothed Cognition." Egyptian Journal of Medical Human Genetics, Elsevier, 21 Feb. 2012, www.sciencedirect.com/science/article/pii/S0022103112000200.

[lxxxvii] "Dress Code or Not, What You Wear Matters." The Fast Track, 6 June 2018, www.quickbase.com/blog/dress-code-or-not-what-you-wear-matters.

[lxxxviii] Hewlett, Ann. "Dress for the Job You Want?" Harvard Business Review, 23 July 2014, hbr.org/2011/02/dress-for-the-job-you-want.

[lxxxix] TodayShow. "Gray Hair's in Fashion, but What about at Work?" TODAY.com, Msnbc.com Contributor, www.today.com/news/gray-hairs-fashion-what-about-work-wbna46928421.

[xc] "These Are the Women CEOs Leading Fortune 500 Companies." Yahoo! Finance, Yahoo!, finance.yahoo.com/news/women-ceos-leading-fortune-500-113001750.html.

[xci] Alsop, Ronald. "Capital – Fat People Earn Less and Have a Harder Time Finding Work." BBC News, BBC, 1 Dec. 2016, www.bbc.com/capital/story/20161130-fat-people-earn-less-and-have-a-harder-time-finding-work.

[xcii] Flint, Stuart W., et al. *Advances in Pediatrics.*, U.S. National Library of Medicine, 2016, www.ncbi.nlm.nih.gov/pmc/articles/PMC4853419/.

[xciii] Lebowitz, Shana. "Science Says People Determine Your Competence, Intelligence, and Salary Based on Your Weight." Business Insider, Business Insider, 9 Sept. 2015, www.businessinsider.com/science-overweight-people-less-successful-2015-9.

[xciv] Coleman, Lauren DeLisa. "Can You Get Away With The No Makeup Trend At Work?" Inc.com, Inc., 17 July 2017, www.inc.com/lauren-delisa-coleman/will-this-big-new-trend-punish-working-women.html.

[xcv] Rosa Silverman. "Bosses Admit They Would Discriminate against Women Not Wearing Makeup." The Telegraph, Telegraph Media Group, 17 Oct. 2013, www.telegraph.co.uk/women/10385501/Bosses-admit-they-would-discriminate-against-women-not-wearing-makeup.html.

[xcvi] "Seventy-One Percent of Employers Say They Value Emotional Intelligence over IQ, According to CareerBuilder Survey." CareerBuilder.ca, www.careerbuilder.ca/share/aboutus/pressreleasesdetail.aspx?id=pr652&sd=8%2F18%2F2011&ed=8%2F18%2F2099.

[xcvii] Macy Bayern. "These Colleges Produce More Fortune 500 CEOs than Any Others." TechRepublic. N.p., n.d. Web. 13 Jan. 2019.

[xcviii] Acostigan. "Statistical Overview of Women in the Workforce." Catalyst, 4 June 2018,

www.catalyst.org/knowledge/statistical-overview-women-workforce.

[xcix] Hamori, Monica, and Boyak Koyunku. "EXPERIENCE MATTERS? THE IMPACT OF PRIOR CEO EXPERIENCE ON FIRM PERFORMANCE." N.p., 2014. Web. 2018.

[c] Savitz, Eric. "The Path To Becoming A Fortune 500 CEO." Forbes, Forbes Magazine, 15 Dec. 2011, www.forbes.com/sites/ciocentral/2011/12/05/the-path-to-becoming-a-fortune-500-ceo/2/#370ec0295d7d.

[ci] "The Benefits of Being Adaptable." *Business.com*, www.business.com/articles/how-well-do-you-handle-change-the-benefits-of-being-adaptable/.

[cii] Bradberry, Travis. "9 Things That Will Kill Your Career." Inc.com, Inc., 28 Apr. 2017, www.inc.com/travis-bradberry/9-things-that-will-kill-your-career.html.

[ciii] "Chapter 2: Equal Treatment for Men and Women." Pew Research Center's Social & Demographic Trends Project, 11 Dec. 2013, www.pewsocialtrends.org/2013/12/11/chapter-2-equal-treatment-for-men-and-women/.

[civ] Forbes, Forbes Magazine, www.forbes.com/forbes/welcome/?toURL=https%3A%2F%2Fwww.forbes.com%2F2003%2F03%2F31%2Fcx_wt_0401exec&refURL=https%3A%2F%2Fwww.google.com%2F&referrer=https%3A%2F%2Fwww.google.com%2F.

[cv] "CEO Genome – Data Driven Insights from GhSMART into What Makes Successful CEOs."CEO Genome, ceogenome.com/.

[cvi] Stillman, Jessica. "You'll Never Guess the Average Age of Successful Silicon Valley Founders." Inc.com, Inc., 8 Dec. 2017,

www.inc.com/jessica-stillman/youll-never-guess-average-age-of-successful-silicon-valley-founders.html.

cvii "12 Reasons to Stop Multitasking." Health.com, www.health.com/health/gallery/0,,20707868,00.html.

cviii Lastoe, Stacey. "This Is Nuts: It Takes Nearly 30 Minutes to Refocus After You Get Distracted." Free Career Advice, The Muse, 11 July 2017, www.themuse.com/advice/this-is-nuts-it-takes-nearly-30-minutes-to-refocus-after-you-get-distracted.

END

Made in the USA
San Bernardino, CA
17 May 2019